FIRST-TIME
LEADER

FIRST-TIME
LEADER

Foundational Tools for
Inspiring and **Enabling** Your New Team

GEORGE BRADT
and
GILLIAN DAVIS

WILEY

Published by John Wiley & Sons, Inc., Hoboken, New Jersey.
Published simultaneously in Canada.

For general information about our other products and services, please contact our Customer Care Department within the United States at (800) 762-2974, outside the United States at (317) 572-3993 or fax (317) 572-4002.

Wiley publishes in a variety of print and electronic formats and by print-on-demand. Some material included with standard print versions of this book may not be included in e-books or in print-on-demand. If this book refers to media such as a CD or DVD that is not included in the version you purchased, you may download this material at http://booksupport.wiley.com. For more information about Wiley products, visit www.wiley.com.

ISBN 978-1-118-82812-0 (cloth); ISBN 978-1-118-85836-3 (ebk); ISBN 978-1-118-85838-7 (ebk)

Printed in the United States of America

10 9 8 7 6 5 4 3 2 1

CONTENTS

NOTE

The 48 tools printed in this book are also available in a customizable format at www.onboardingtools.com. (See the First-Time Leader page.) We will be regularly updating these tools and adding videos and additional material on that page to give you the benefit of our latest thinking.

ACKNOWLEDGMENTS

Gillian sat at her desk. She had just become responsible for a small team of six—all of whom had been there a lot longer than she had and were a generation ahead of her. She knew what she wanted to accomplish; she just didn't know how to get there.

She picked up George's *The New Leader's 100-Day Action Plan* to find some guidance. Although very insightful, she found a lot of it was over her head, as she was not leading an organization but a small team. So she called him.

"George, just read your *The New Leader's 100-Day Action Plan* book. Really great stuff, but do you have anything for first-time leaders?"

"Thanks. Not at the moment. Why do you ask?"

"Well, I know a lot of people who are first-time leaders—they are either in a high-growth organization and are quickly building a team underneath them, are start-up owners that are expanding, or are in corporate and are being promoted without the right, or any, leadership training. Even in my own experience, I could really use a book to help me be not just a manager but a leader."

"I think you're right. Do you want to fill that gap together?"

"Yes."

And we were off to the races.

This book has many other roots. It is a direct descendant of *The New Leader's 100-Day Action Plan*, written with Jayme Check and Jorge Pedraza. Large portions were taken from other things George has written. We've referenced the specific articles "adapted" from Forbes.com, but not the pieces from *The New Leader's 100-Day Action Plan* or from the book *Onboarding* that George wrote with Mary Vonnegut or from *The Total Onboarding Program* that George wrote with Ed Bancroft. So thank you Ed, Jayme, Jorge, and Mary for your contributions.

Beyond them we must acknowledge the contributions of our past and current partners in PrimeGenesis. Their fingerprints are all over this book and all our books as we all work these ideas every day.

As always, we are indebted to the clients of PrimeGenesis and Alan Davis & Associates Inc. on several levels. We are the first to admit that we have learned as much from them as they have from us. We are blessed to have the opportunity to work with an extremely diverse group of clients. They run the gamut from the multinational to the small, public to the private, for-profit to the not-for-profit.

The leaders we work with come from many industries, from almost every discipline imaginable, and from many parts of the world. With every client, we have learned something new. Clients inspire, challenge, and teach us on a daily basis, and for that we are grateful.

To Meg, who seems to greet every one of George's new initiatives—from businesses to books to musical plays and everything in between—with a bemused look of "Oh no. Not again" and ends up supporting everything he does in a way no one else on the planet could begin to come close to, abounding gratitude.

To Gillian's parents, who gave her a platform to stand on, and to Kudzi, for enabling her to reach her dreams.

GETTING STARTED

OVERVIEW: CONGRATULATIONS! IT'S GREAT TO BE A LEADER. YOU'VE EARNED IT. AND YOUR NEW JOB IS GOING TO BE A WILD RIDE

PART I: GETTING STARTED

"If only I had known then what I know now about leadership." Our vision is that years from now, this thought will never cross your mind. Most people become good leaders only after stumbling through new situations, making mistakes, and learning from them. Not you. You're going to benefit from several lifetimes of leadership insights, learning from others' mistakes and positive experiences to cut out a lot of unnecessary stumbling and pain and accelerate your success as a first-time leader.

Before we go any further, congratulations! If you're reading this, either you have earned a career-defining opportunity, or you are wise enough to reconnect with the fundamentals of leadership with fresh eyes. You should be excited. And you should temper that excitement with a healthy dose of concern. Your opportunity comes with a fair degree of personal risk. Forty percent of new leaders fail in their first 18 months.[1] That's why this book is for you. It's going help you mitigate the risks and accelerate success all at the same time.

When Gillian first started her role as manager, she went in with guns blazing. She assumed the best way to get people to buy into her ideas was to prove that she was capable. So she went off in all directions, trying to change processes, marketing plans, new product lines. It wasn't long before she realized that not only was this not working, it wasn't sustainable. She needed to be strategic, and most importantly, patient.

The number one problem first-time leaders face is failing to understand that leading requires entirely different strengths than does doing or managing. We've all experienced first-time managers who come in with guns blazing. They think they can be successful by doing more of what they were doing before and telling others to do the same. But telling diminishes. At best people comply with the teller's direction. More experienced managers persuade and support. Great leaders go one step further to co-create a purpose-driven future with their followers.

This gets us to our core premises:

- **Leading is different from managing.** Where managing is about organizing, coordinating, and telling, leading is about inspiring and enabling and co-creating. Great leaders can also do and tell when needed—and we're certainly going to provide you a broad set of management tools—but this is not a book written to help you write a budget or comply with labor laws. It is a book about leadership with a focus on inspiring and enabling others to do their absolute best together to realize a meaningful and rewarding shared purpose.
- **Taking over as a leader for the first time is a critical, career-defining moment.** Getting this transition right accelerates your career trajectory. Avoiding avoidable mistakes at this juncture requires preparation, commitment, and follow-through. Hence this book.
- **Focus on the cause.** People follow charismatic leaders for a time. But they devote themselves over time to the cause of a BRAVE leader who inspires and enables them in the pursuit of that cause. BRAVE leaders have the courage to accept that leadership is not about them, but rather about working through behaviors, relationships, attitude, values, and the environment to inspire and enable others.

This book provides foundational frameworks, processes, and tools to help by

- Laying out a way of thinking and a structure for action for your leadership at both conceptual and tactical levels. We'll tell you what to do next, later, never, and why, and how to accelerate success.
- Providing several lifetimes of leadership insights, examples, and stories from experienced leaders and experts to guide you through risk-filled situations you may not have experienced yourself—yet.
- Making available downloadable tools, easily adaptable for the situations you face. (Plus bonus tools and new ideas over time, online at www .onboardingtools.com.)

Happiness is good. Actually, three goods: (1) doing good for others, (2) doing things you're good at, and (3) doing good for you. These three goods come together in great leaders. Great leadership flows from a passion for a cause—inevitably a cause with a meaningful impact on others. At the same time, these leaders invest in making themselves ever better leaders on an ongoing basis. As a result, they reap abundant personal rewards: good for others, good at it, good for you.

There are real costs to becoming and being a great leader. Assuming you've got the talent and inclination to lead (and not all do), you need to invest in acquiring knowledge and skills. It's a never-ending effort. You are going to be frustrated along the way. You are going to make tough choices, giving up some personal comfort in pursuit of your cause. You are going to be stressed. You are going to fail. Then you are going to get up and do it all over again. Why? Because the impact and rewards far more than offset the investment and costs.

We are going to give you a process for taking charge, a framework for leadership, and then apply those across small, medium, and large teams to accelerate success. Here's the flow by chapter for the chapters following this one.

Take Charge of Your New Team

When moving into that first-time leadership role, get a head start, manage your message, build your team. Get a head start by having a plan and putting an emphasis on jump-starting relationships. Manage your message by making sure what you do matches what you say matches what you fundamentally believe. Then apply the components of the BRAVE leadership success framework to build your team.

The BRAVE Leadership Success Framework: Behaviors, Relationships, Attitudes, Values, Environment

Behaviors are the actions that make real, lasting impact on others.
Relationships are the heart of leadership. If you can't connect, you can't lead.
Attitude encompasses strategic, posture, and culture choices around how to win.
Values are the bedrock of a high-performing team. Get clear on what really matters and why.
Environment sets the context for everything else in terms of where you are playing.

PART II: BUILD YOUR BRAVE LEADERSHIP FROM THE OUTSIDE IN

Behaviors flow from relationships. But you can't get there until you're aligned on environment, values, and attitude choices. Thus we suggest leading from the outside in: from the environment, through values and attitudes, to relationships and behaviors. As a first-time leader, it's hard to know where to start; you have expectations coming at you from all angles: your boss, your boss's boss, your peers, your team. If you don't build yourself a platform to stand on, you will not be able to stand for long.

Environment: Get Clear on Your Mission and Fields of Action

One of your most important choices is where to play. Understand the context in which you're operating and interpret and create the context for your team. The context includes both what others have decided for you and the choices you and your team get to make. Today's environment is highly uncertain in exciting and dangerous ways. So be sure to consider all the risks and opportunities both outside and inside your field of endeavor and organization. You may never have had to consider the external environment in your previous role, but now it's your responsibility to do your homework.

- Understand the business and competitive environment, organizational history, and recent results.
- Align around an interpretation of the situation assessment.
- Make clear choices around where to play and where not to play within your context.

Values: Align Yourself and Your Team with the Organization's Mission, Vision, and Values—More or Less

Virtually every long-serving leader says that the number one job of a leader at any level is to own and drive vision, mission, and values. Clarify what matters and why—the value you and your team create, and the drivers and principles you choose to follow within the context of the overall organization. All too often, this exercise is overlooked. Just because your manager did not do this, does not mean you should skip it as well.

- Align on a shared purpose: vision, mission, values as the foundation for all that follows.

Attitude: Make Crucial Choices around your Team's Strategy, Posture, and Culture

Strategy, posture, and culture comprise the pivot point between environment and values and relationships and behaviors. Decide how you are going to fulfill the mission you've been given—how you are going to win. To change your organization's behaviors and relationships, change its attitude. Make choices around strategy (which may be someone else's substrategy) and then be sure your posture and culture are in sync with those choices.

- Clarify strategy, posture, and culture to guide relationships and behaviors.

Relationships: The Heart of Leadership

Everything you do and don't do, say and don't say, listen to, and observe communicates—24/7, forever. This is the heart of leadership. Inspiring and enabling others is all about relationships. This is probably the biggest shift for first-time leaders. At least it was for Gillian. Shifting from executing the work to delegating the work was one of her biggest challenges, and continues to be one. You are changing habits and doing a 180-degree change on how you perceive your role. This doesn't happen overnight, and you'll be happy to have the tools in this book to keep you on track.

- MAP your communication: Message, Amplifiers, Perseverance.
- Build an ADEPT team by Acquiring, Developing, Encouraging, Planning, and Transitioning talent over time.

Behaviors: How You Get Things Done through Other People

Environment, values, attitude, and relationships all inform behaviors and what impact you and your team make. It's all theoretical gibberish until you put it into action. Remember that activity is not the same as impact. So focus everyone on those few behaviors with the greatest impact.

- Focus the team on what creates the most value for your team's internal and external customers across the value chain: design–build–sell–deliver–support.[2]

PART III: LEADING SMALL, MEDIUM, AND LARGE TEAMS

Mange teams differently as they grow.

With Teams of Less Than 10 People, Adopt a Start-Up Mind-Set

If you are starting or joining a small team, lead with environment and values. The critical questions are where to play and what matters. Build everything else on these over time. Play where you can solve someone's problem. Then assemble your early team of complementary partners. Not everyone on the team needs to have strategic, operational, and organizational strengths. But someone on the team should, and all must buy into the same values.

- Play where you can solve someone's problem and build the strengths required to solve that problem either in your early team or through external partners.
- Lock in core values.
- Gain early momentum and keep going until it's time to stop.

Lead Teams of 10 to 20 Like an Extended Family

Once the team grows beyond a nuclear family with everyone reporting to one leader, the nature of how the team works changes. At this point, attitude starts to become more important. Get the strategy set, deciding at what you are going to be best in the world, and use that as your guide for how to grow the team and which capabilities to add first. With teams of 10 to 30 people or so, you'll know everyone and can treat them like extended family. Even so, this is the time to implement rudimentary people-management and operating practices.

- Choose what you are going to be best in the world at.
- Let that choice guide team expansion priorities.
- Agree on the main tenets of your culture and start implementing operational practices to embed those tenets.

If You're Leading More Than 30 People, Hierarchy Is Your Friend

While it's not likely your first leadership team will have more than 30, it does happen. The more likely scenario is that you start with a smaller team and grow it. Once your team has more than 30 people, you need to get over your natural abhorrence of hierarchy and start substituting some organizational and operating processes for your ability to know everyone on the team. With this size team, lead with relating and behaviors (how to connect, what impact). Work on the organization. Put in place enabling practices to scale. And remember the number one job of the leader is to own and reinforce vision and values. This gets ever more important (and complicated) as the organization grows.

- Work on the organization.
- Put in place enabling practices to scale.
- Reinforce vision and values—the number one job of a leader.

Call them what you want: moments of truth, moments of opportunity, moments of impact. Whatever you call them, leadership and life itself is a series of them. Whether planned, unplanned, seen, unseen, known, or unknown, they go by in a flash. This is especially true for first-time leaders in their first interactions with their new team members, their first tough decisions, their first hires, fires, failures, and successes.

To capture those moments, to take full advantage of those opportunities, engage with the prelude ahead of the moment, the moment of impact itself, and the follow-through after the moment. The BRAVE framework applies. During the prelude, think through environment (where to play), values (what matters), and attitude (how to win). This sets you up for the moment of impact and relating to others (how to connect). Then follow through to ensure all focus on those few behaviors with the greatest impact (what impact).

Leaders are defined by their followers. The only way to achieve your vision, in line with your values, in the context you choose, is through the attitude, relationships, and behaviors you model and engender in your followers. It's not about you. It's about your cause. It's not enough to have compliant followers, doing what they must. It's not even enough to have contributing followers. You need followers committed to a deserving cause. Be BRAVE yourself and help them be BRAVE individually and together in a winning BRAVE culture.

Throughout, our emphasis is on the application of principles. This is a book and set of tools to be used and referenced, not something to be read through, considered, and put aside. Note, the 48 tools printed in this book are also available in a customizable format at www.onboardingtools.com (see the First-Time Leader page). We will be regularly updating these tools and adding videos and additional material on that page to give you the benefit of our latest thinking. Finally, just as you as a first-time leader must inspire and enable others, we hope to inspire and enable you to be a BRAVE leader this time and every time.

Chapter 2

TAKE CHARGE OF YOUR NEW TEAM

MOVING INTO YOUR FIRST LEADERSHIP ROLE FROM OUTSIDE

As George and his coauthors first said in their book *The New Leader's 100-Day Action Plan*, over the years, we have noticed that many first-time leaders show up for a new role happy and smiling, but without a plan. Neither they nor their organizations have thought things through in advance. On their first day, they are welcomed by such confidence-building remarks as "Oh, you're here . . . we'd better find you an office."

Unacceptable.

Gillian was thrust into her first leadership role with short notice. Like many first-time leaders she found herself on day 1 with no plan, a long list of goals, and no clue where and what to start, how to delegate, or how to communicate to her new team. She spent her first few days in her office, writing out plans and strategies. She knows now, the last place she should have been was behind her desk.

Some enlightened organizations have a better process in place. If you are lucky, you will be associated with an organization that actually puts people in charge of preparing for a leader's transition into a new role. Imagine the difference when new leaders are escorted to offices that are fully set up for them, complete with computer, passwords, phones, files, information, and a 30-day schedule of orientation and assimilation meetings.

Better . . . but still not good enough. Even if the company has done this for you, if you have waited until this moment to start, you are already behind, and you have stacked the odds against yourself. Paradoxically, the best way to accelerate a transition into a new leadership role is to pause long enough to think through a plan and put it in place—and then get a head start on implementing it.

George and his partners started PrimeGenesis in 2003 having noticed the difference between leaders who have a plan, hit the ground running, and make an impact on their first day, and leaders who wait until day 1 to start planning. Since then, PrimeGenesis has created and deployed a set of tools and techniques that help leaders quickly and effectively transition into new roles. Their clients (and new leaders who follow the principles in this book) get better results faster and reduce their failure rate from 40 percent to less than 10 percent at large, small, and not-for-profit organizations.

PrimeGenesis' three main ideas are

1. **Get a head start.** Day 1 is a critical moment of impact for people joining from outside the company. The same is true for the formal announcement of someone getting promoted or transferred from within. In each of these situations, you can accelerate progress by getting a head start and hitting the ground running. Preparation breeds confidence and a little early momentum goes a long way.
2. **Manage the message.** Everything communicates. People read things into everything you say and do, and everything you don't say and don't do. You're far better off choosing and guiding what others see and hear, and when they see and hear it, rather than letting happenstance or others make those choices for you.
3. **Build the team.** You will fail if you try to do everything yourself, without the support and buy-in of your team. As a first-time leader, your own success is inextricably linked to the success of the team as a whole. And no one is going to follow you until you have earned the right to lead. You must converge into the team before you can lead the team.

George's first book, *The New Leader's 100-Day Action Plan* lays out a very specific program for leaders taking over relatively large teams. Here we're going to propose a more general program for first-time leaders of teams of any size. But before we get into the program itself, let's talk about risk management.

Risk Management on the Way to a New Role

The most opportune time to complete your due diligence is between the offer and acceptance phases. Waiting until later or ignoring this step hurts your potential for success. Make sure that the job is right for you. Mitigate organization, role, and personal risks by answering the questions outlined in Tool 2.1.

Sometimes we fall into the trap of feeling that we should take a role because it's what others expect us do to. Don't do that. Make your own choices or you will fail, burn out, or, worse, be generally unhappy eventually. Answer these questions honestly, before you move on.

In assessing these risks, three steps can help:

1. Leverage and supplement Tool 2.1's questions about the company, the team, your new boss(es), and the major challenges and objectives you and the organization will face.
2. Identify potential sources of information: scouts, seconds, and spies across customers, collaborators, capabilities, competitors, and conditions.
3. Gather and analyze the information.

TOOL 2.1
ONBOARDING RISK ASSESSMENT

Following are key questions to answer during due diligence to help mitigate risk.

Mitigate Organizational Risk
1. What is the organization's sustainable competitive advantage?
2. Are there any risks with the current *customer* base?
3. Are there any risks with relationships with significant *collaborators* of the organization?
4. Does the organization have the *capabilities* required for long-term success?
5. Do *competitors* pose significant risks to the viability of the organization?
6. Are there any outside *conditions* that will impact the viability of the organization?

Mitigate Role Risk
1. Did anyone have concerns about this role and, if so, what was done to mitigate them?
2. Why does the position exist? Why did they need to create it in the first place?
3. What are the objectives and outcomes? What are you supposed to get done?
4. What will the impact be on the rest of the organization? What kind of interactions can you expect with key stakeholders?
5. What are your specific responsibilities, including decision-making authority and direct reports?

Mitigate Personal Risk
1. What, specifically, about me led the organization to offer me the job?
2. Is this the company and role that can best capitalize on my strengths over time?
3. Will I look forward to coming to work three weeks, months, or years from now?
4. Will I fit with the culture?

(continued)

Overall Risk Assessment	
If You Are Facing	**You Should**
A low level of risk	Do nothing out of the ordinary (but keep your eyes open for inevitable changes).
Manageable risk	Manage it in the normal course of your job.
Mission-crippling risk	Resolve it before accepting the job, or mitigate it before doing anything else if you are already in the job.
Insurmountable barriers	Walk away.

Copyright © PrimeGenesis® LLC. To customize this document, download Tool 2.1 from the First-Time Leader page on www.onboardingtools.com.

With that in mind, let's walk through the steps of BRAVE onboarding and pull them together into Tool 2.2. The core components are thinking through where to play, what matters, and how to win before you start, connecting with others to build relationships through your start, and making the right choices about impact you will make throughout.

Note *onboarding* is the term we use to refer to moving into a new role. It comes from the formal ceremony in which a new captain comes on board a ship to take charge.

Environment—Where to Play

Learn about the historical context, business and competitive environment, and recent results. Don't be afraid to ask. Then think through the implications of those for your particular situation. As a first-time leader, put a particular emphasis on the history of the team's leaders, getting at what worked particularly well and less well. The 5Cs situational analysis and SWOT tools will give you a framework to think about customers, collaborators, capabilities, competitors, and conditions and strengths, weaknesses, opportunities, and threats respectively.

Values—What Matters

Learn about the current mission, vision, and values. You'll be relooking at them later. But start with what's already in place. As a first-time leader, concentrate on evolving what the team is already thinking instead of imposing your going-in thoughts.

Attitude—How to Win

Learn about the current strategy, posture, and culture as part of your own converging into the organization and team. Do this as a first-time leader by probing stakeholders up, down, and across and observing what's going on before trying to change things.

Relationships—How to Connect

This is where the generalities stop. This is the heart of leadership. Think through what you're going to say and not say, do and not do in great detail so you don't make some of the obvious missteps.

Start by identifying the names/titles of the few most critical stakeholders:

Up: Your boss, his or her boss, and any other people that can tell you what to do
Across: Internal peers, external and internal customers, external and internal suppliers
Down: Direct reports, perhaps some indirect reports
Former: (if promoted from within) Up, across, down stakeholders from former role

Think through your message and communication plan:

Platform for change: Note what will make your audience realize they need to change.
Vision: Picture a brighter future—that your audience can see themselves in.
Call to action: Note actions the audience can take.
Headline: Note short phrase that conveys the essence of your message (bumper sticker length).
Amplifiers: Note the people and things that will convey and amplify your message.
Media: Lay out which media to use.
Steps: Note the steps of your communication plan.

Clarify fuzzy front-end/prestart steps. The fuzzy front end is the golden time between when you accept the job and actually start. This is where you get a head start by preparing and starting to jump-start relationships.

Personal setup: Note things to get family set and basic office accommodations.
Jump-start learning: Note information to gather and digest.
Conversations: Determine the few most critical stakeholders to meet live/by phone before day 1. (Rank your stakeholders from most important to least important, meeting with them live before your start, calling them before

your start, meeting them early after your start, meeting them later, or avoiding them as warranted.)

During these first conversations, focus on building the relationships first. You may want to ask about their perceptions of the situation and the organization's strengths and capabilities, about priorities and resources, about the culture, and about the best way to communicate with them.

Announcement cascade: Lay out who will hear what, when, how in advance of an announcement; how an announcement will be made; and who will hear what, when, how after an announcement.

Day 1/early days: Lay out specific actions for day 1—whom to meet with, when, what forum. What signals to send/how to reinforce message (see earlier discussion). Complete the same for the early days.

Pivot: Determine how to pivot from converging to evolving in creating a high-performing team. This is going to be different depending upon the size of your team and situation. Sometimes you'll want to lay out the new imperative. Sometimes you'll want to consult with your team. Sometimes you'll want to co-create it with your team in some sort of imperative workshop. Either way, figure out how and when to pivot.

Behaviors—What Impact

Work across three processes: operational, organizational, and strategic.

Operational: Determine initial operating process/cadence including periodic operational meetings to manage milestones and timing to determine early wins.

Organizational: Determine initial organizational processes across acquiring, developing, encouraging, planning, and transitioning talent.

Strategic: Determine initial strategic process/cadence across quarters. You may find it helpful to do a talent review in Q1, a strategic plan in Q2, succession planning in Q3 flowing from the strategic plan, and then operating plans in Q4.

TOOL 2.2
BRAVE ONBOARDING

Preparation/Learning/Plan

Environment—Where to Play
Historical context:
Business environment (5Cs, SWOT):
Recent results:
Implications for where to play:

Values — What Matters
   Mission:
   Vision:
   Values:

Attitude — How to Win
   Strategy:
   Posture:
   Culture:

Relationships — How to Connect
   Stakeholders
      Up:
      Across:
      Down:
      (Former:)
   Message
      Platform for change:
      Vision:
      Call to action:
      Headline:
      Amplifiers:
      Media:
      Steps:

Fuzzy Front End/Prestart

   Personal setup:
   Learning:
   Conversations:
   Announcement cascade:

Day 1/Early Days

Pivot (imperative workshop?)

Behaviors — What Impact
   Operational process/cadence (milestones, early wins):
   Organizational process:
   Strategic processes/cadence (talent–strategic–succession–operating plans):

We're going to illustrate many of our points with stories. These stories feature people from junior to very senior leaders. Don't get hung up on titles, levels, or specifics that are not directly applicable to your current situation. Instead, focus on the underlying lesson.

Jennifer went from a human resources coordinator role, with one direct report, to HR manager at an e-learning business with a team of 40. She recognized early on that the key to success was to connect, as she had to build trust—and fast. She had the luxury of having one-on-one meetings with every team member. At those meetings she made sure she was listening and they were talking. She also met with the strategy team early on to get a clear idea of the team's strengths, weaknesses, opportunities, and threats, and the vision.

Jennifer's takeaways for first-time leaders:

- Stay organized by always having a plan.
- Everything you do has to be aligned with the business strategy.
- Focus on relationships to build up your credibility. This is especially important if you want to make changes.

Why Preparing in Advance Is Priceless: How MasterCard CEO Ajay Banga Planned Ahead for His New Leadership Role[1]

Ajay Banga did a particularly good job at MasterCard at embracing and leveraging his fuzzy front end (the time between the acceptance of the job and his start date). Many leaders fall into the trap of believing that leadership begins on day 1 of a new job, but Banga's actions are a good example of how leaders can use the time before then to get a head start in order to increase their chance of success.

Making the Move to MasterCard CEO

Ajay's transition from Citibank to MasterCard began even before the official announcement in June 2009 that he would join the company that summer. Arguably, his whole initial role as COO was one large fuzzy front end before he took over as CEO on July 1, 2010.

Ajay explained to George that this was all part of the three-stage plan created by his predecessor, Bob Selander, and the board: stage 1—Ajay as COO reporting to Bob; stage 2—Ajay as CEO with Bob still around; and stage 3—Ajay as CEO with Bob not there.

Looking back on the transition, Ajay said Bob did a "masterful" job at allowing him to settle in and pick up pieces step-by-step without all the external and internal pressures getting dumped on him at the same time.

Throughout, Ajay leveraged his leadership skills in connecting with people. After 13 years at Citibank, he had an insider's view of the way things worked there.

Ajay explained that it "gets in your blood through a sort of reverse osmosis. . . . But at MasterCard, I'm the outsider. So the only way I could get up to speed on the culture, what's working, what's not working, our competitive strengths and the like was to invest in listening."

Thus, he spent a lot of time doing just that. Ajay describes walking into offices at the headquarters, sitting down (or "flopping in a chair") and saying, "I'm Ajay. Tell me about yourself." or "What can I do to help?" or "What should I not do?" Good start, but not good enough. Then Ajay went out to meet "people outside the big offices," traveling around the world to visit MasterCard's country offices to learn about their obstacles and strengths.

This is a great example of how to connect. You may not have the influence or contact with the board, but you do have your team. Listen to your team. Do walk around to connect with them, and make sure they are doing the talking. Encourage open lines of communication by making your team feel comfortable sharing how they feel or their ideas.

Actions to Take between Acceptance of a Job and the Start Date

This is a good example of the value of investing in relationships even before the start. There's no doubt that holding conversations with critical stakeholders before day 1 is a good thing. We used to think that was because the leader was more in control of his or her time before he or she had to deal with the day-to-day demands of the job. While that's still true, Brene Brown has helped George understand the Power of Vulnerability in connecting people.[2] Asking for help before the start is such an act of vulnerability.

> Implications for you: Take advantage of the time between when you accept the job and actually start.

Powerful First Impressions: Michael Brune's Day 1 at the Sierra Club[3]

Michael Brune took control of his first day as executive director of the Sierra Club. At least he took control of the things he could control. While he was not able to alter his 18-month-old son's sleep habits the night before so he could be well rested, he did use available media to start communicating his message at work immediately—a critical component of transition management.

Owning Day 1

As Brune explained to George, he took time out before he started to research the organization's history and think through what he wanted to get done on first day, first week, and first month.

> Since I knew I was going to go deep underwater, I wanted to have just a couple of big priorities that I wanted to stick to for at least the first month. . . . Having those touchstones helped me to bring a little bit of order into the chaos of starting a new job.

Those touchstones included these three:

1. Being more solutions oriented. "For years we'd been good at stopping (bad) things." Now it seemed to be important to help move good things forward on "symbolic and substantive ways."
2. "Pull[ing] out what our bottom lines were"—the things on which they could not compromise on as a way to provide a backstop beyond which they could not go.
3. Modernizing the club, utilizing technology, and polishing the brand to be more energetic, and so on.

On his first day, Brune wrote in his blog,

> Today's my first day. I'm inspired and honored to be a part of such a dem-ocratically-governed, volunteer-powered organization. From helping to protect Yosemite and millions of acres of wilderness to the more recent work of building powerful alliances with labor and impacted communi-ties, Sierra Club volunteers and staff have played a pivotal role in many of the most important environmental victories over the past century.
>
> But as effective as the organization has been over the past 118 years, we need to do our best work in the years ahead. The challenges—and opportunities—are too great.

Brune did several things right:

- He switched his identity and allegiance instantly, talking about himself as part of his new organization.
- He credited his predecessors and current team, telling people he hoped to follow their examples and build on their "victories."
- He started driving his message and communication points with what he said and what he did, wearing his own passion for the environment on his sleeve.

- He started by listening instead of "talking, pontificating, declaring." His first morning he met with his team to get an update on what they were doing and connect with work they'd already done. He learned where they thought the organization was strong and where they thought it needed help.
- Then, after listening to the team and taking that in, he had an all-staff, multi-office meeting to introduce himself to all and lay out his own initial observations about places needing attention.

How to Plan Ahead for Day 1

As you plan your own day 1, here are a couple of things to keep in mind:

- **It is personal.** As a leader, you impact peoples' lives. Those people will try very hard to figure out you and your potential impact as soon as they can. They may even rush to judgment. Keep that in mind at all times.
- **Order counts.** Be circumspect about the order in which you meet with people and the timing of when you do what throughout day 1 and your early days.
- **Messages matter.** Have a message. Know what you are going to say and not say. Have a bias toward listening, and avoid directing. Know that strong opinions, long-winded introductions, and efforts to prove yourself immediately are rarely, if ever, good day 1 tactics. People will be looking to form opinions early. Keep that in mind while deciding when to listen, when to share, what to ask, who to ask, and how you answer. When speaking keep it brief, on point, and meaningful.
- **Location counts.** Think about where you will show up for work on day 1. Do not just show up at your designated office by default.
- **Signs and symbols count.** Be aware of all the ways in which you communicate, well beyond just words.
- **Timing counts.** Day 1 does not have to match the first day you get paid. Decide which day you want to communicate as day 1 to facilitate other choices about order and location.

Implications for you: Manage your message, keeping in mind that everything communicates.

Don't Lead until You Have Earned the Right to Lead in a New Job[4]

"About 40 percent of leaders who change jobs or get promoted fail in the first 18 months." As Anne Fisher points out in a recent *Fortune* article, this has been true for about 15 years.[5]

A big reason for the ongoing failure rate is the inability of new leaders to determine the right time to pivot from *converging* (becoming part of the team) to *evolving* (initiating change) when they are moving into a new organization, changing jobs, or getting promoted—and the inability of others to help them get this timing right.

Let's unpack that into three musts for new leaders:

1. Must adopt a converge and evolve approach to taking charge
2. Must make a conscious choice about pivoting from converging to evolving
3. Must time that pivot right

Must Converge and Evolve

We use an ACES approach to onboarding, in which leaders make a choice based on the business context and corporate culture of the company whether to Assimilate in, Converge and Evolve, or Shock a system by making immediate changes.

Understand that while there are certainly some situations where it's right to shock a system or simply assimilate in, in the vast majority of cases, converging and evolving is the right approach. New leaders cannot lead until they have established a working relationship with their followers. Hence, converge and evolve.

As noted earlier, Ajay Banga did this particularly well when he went into MasterCard.

Must Choose to Pivot

Converging and evolving are different. The activities are different. The skills utilized are different. This is why a new leader can't do both at the same time. This is why it's so important to have a clear pivot point between asking/converging and leading/evolving.

QlikTech's Lars Bjork used his first annual meeting to do this, and it worked so well that he pulls his whole company together every year to pivot from the learnings of the year before to the priorities of the year ahead.

Must Time Your Pivot Right

There is no one right time for your pivot. Indeed, you may need to time your pivot differently with different teams, but there are some guidelines that may be helpful.

Normal Timing

Normal pivot timing is toward the end of your first month in a new job. If you leverage the time frame between accepting a job and starting it, what we call the fuzzy front end, to jump-start some of your most important relationships, you can use most of your first month to listen, learn, and get up to speed on what's really happening in your new role. This should allow you to know enough to have a productive pivot session by the end of the month.

Another advantage of pivoting toward the end of your first month is that most organizations operate on monthly cycles. They have standing monthly meetings. They do monthly reports. Thus, having some sort of imperative workshop or other event to pivot from converging to evolving at this point puts it within your first full cycle with the organization, heightening its sense of urgency.

[Gillian spent her first month acting like a sponge, absorbing as much as she could from others. She listened to employees, clients, and competitors, and at the end of month one, she pivoted. She had a good lay of the land to know what had to be done, who had to do it, and how they were going to get there. She needed the first month of absorbing to know what was right.]

Accelerated Timing

You will need to pivot earlier if the context demands it. Expect this in start-up or turnaround situations. Ideally, you can shift the whole time line forward by getting an earlier start on your fuzzy front end. If you can't do this, do what you can to accelerate the building of relationships before you pivot. Know that pivoting early puts stress on the organization and be prepared to deal with that. If you find yourself in a case like this, how to connect becomes even more important to you.

Delayed Timing

You will want to pivot later if the culture and context are conducive to that. Expect this to be the case if things are going well and there's more downside to breaking what's working than upside to initiating new ideas. Do watch out for the boss who tells you to take your time converging into the culture but wants you to deliver improved results at the same time.

In the final analysis, this is more art than science. Choose to converge first. Choose to evolve next. Choose a point in time to pivot between the two—and then evolve your thinking around that timing as you learn more while converging.

Implications for you: Map out the path from converging to evolving—and timing.

Three Things to Remember When Onboarding into a Smaller Organization[6]

The same three things derail people onboarding into small companies as those onboarding into large companies: poor fit, failure to deliver, and an inability to deal with changes along the way. But the way to deal with those obstacles in smaller companies is different. You must

1. Fit within the organization's broader ecosystem as well as your workgroup.
2. Deliver with fewer resources and less structure.
3. Create change instead of waiting for it to happen.

Val Rahmani was the poster child for both moving from a large to a small company and dealing with risk. She was a 28-year veteran of IBM (which most would consider to be a large company) who moved to cyber-security pioneer Damballa (a small, private company). She dealt with risk every day in her job as CEO and in her free time, as a member of the British aerobatics team.

Rahmani gave George her perspective on the three things to keep in mind when moving to a smaller organization.

Fit with the Organization's Broader Ecosystem

Forty percent of new leaders fail in their first 18 months. The number one reason is poor fit. In a large company, this is about fitting in with your boss, direct reports, and key peers and the culture of the organization. In a small company, external stakeholders like the board, key customers and suppliers, and the community in which you work tend to be much more closely integrated into the functioning of the organization. It's important to fit with them as well. Many moving from large to small companies don't know this. Now you do.

Rahmani experienced this in her move from IBM to Damballa, where she relearned the importance of networking. As she explained to George, at IBM she generally "got introduced" to people. Even if she was making a cold call, her IBM business card turned the call warm in an instant. Without the IBM net, she worked hard to become part of the broader community and of the smaller tech community within Atlanta. The good news was that the "folks in Atlanta were amazing," welcoming and helpful.

Networking can be an important part of your new leader role. Don't underestimate the power of connecting with people in your network. Be smart in choosing what groups or events you go to, and don't burn out on networking events. Quality over quantity. Get to know your external environment through connecting and networking with others.

Gillian was able to grow her search business through a strategic partnership with a contract search firm. Some would see them as competitors, but it was totally collaborative. What Gillian's firm couldn't provide its clients, their partners could, and vice versa. It was great to be able to fill the gaps when meeting a client, instead of leaving the table open to another firm. Gillian's firm was a small business, and to offer what its partner offers would have taken time and a lot of money.

They also believe in sticking to what they know and doing it best. This strategic partnership has allowed for them to grow, and offer more to their clients. This was all down to getting out and networking.

Deliver with Fewer Resources and Less Structure

At one point George stopped hiring people directly out of Procter & Gamble. The trouble was that everyone there knew they could depend on their colleagues to deliver what they promised to deliver when they promised to deliver it. If Manufacturing said it would ship products on May 10, it shipped on May 10. When Finance gave you a set of numbers, they were right. When Market Research said something was true, it was true.

This doesn't always hold in smaller organizations. Groups are stretched thinner. They have to do things faster. They're inventing processes and procedures on the way. Things slip through the cracks. People accustomed to everything working like clockwork often get disoriented the first few times the clocks miss a beat. It turns out that flexibility is a learned skill—and an important one for a small company.

Rahmani doesn't miss IBM's structure at all. She found she could leverage off-the-shelf software solutions for her CRM (Customer Relationship Management) and HR needs, and the lack of structure in her smaller company made it easier to get things done. She thinks "human beings create process" where sometimes none is needed. Sometimes people hesitate to do things because they think they are in violation of a process that doesn't exist. She found herself telling people to "Just tell me (what you think)" instead of inventing a process to slow things down.

Create Instead of Adapt to Change

Darwin told us that survival of the fittest is all about survival of those best able to adapt to change. Almost by definition, larger companies have more moving parts, each of which must adapt to change. If larger companies don't adapt, they get hurt. But it's a whole different game for smaller companies. As Rahmani put it, "We are imposing change on the market." If smaller companies don't create change, there's no reason for them to exist.

Most companies have a product or a service they compete with others to sell to customers. Rahmani's Damballa did all that, but had another dimension—"bad guys." Damballa is in the business of helping organizations stay ahead of malware threats by detecting criminal activity and cyber-threats in their early stages. Rahmani says, "We're at war. We have to be slicker, faster and better to be ahead." If they're not ahead, not creating change, the bad guys will get ahead of them and Damballa will have no value.

Rahmani had a couple of closing thoughts to our discussion: (1) She thinks it would be even harder to move from a small company to a big company. (2) Her advice to people thinking about making the move to a smaller company is "It's a ton of fun. Do it!"

If you do, make sure you fit with the broader group, deliver with less structure, and create change.

Implications for you: Keep the context in mind.

GETTING PROMOTED TO YOUR FIRST LEADERSHIP ROLE FROM WITHIN

The basics of (1) get a head start, (2) manage your message, and (3) build your team apply in every case. What's different when you are promoted from within or laterally transferred is what you need to get a head start on and the restrictions around that, the nature of your message and the context for that message, and the conditions and context of your team building.

Promoted from Within or Lateral Transfer

Consider the successful handoff in a running relay race. The new runner, who's already on the track, does three things: (1) prepares and starts moving in advance; (2) takes control of the transition by putting his hand where he wants the baton placed; and (3) accelerates decisively following the handoff. Those promoted from within or making a lateral transfer should follow the same model.

The basics of new leadership apply whether it's in a new company or the same company. The fundamental difference between moving to a new company and making an internal move, however, is that, in the latter case you are like a relay runner preparing to receive the baton—you are already on the track. Unlike joining an organization for the first time, when you have to create a new positioning for yourself, when you're making an internal move, people already know you or know people that know you. Thus, to a large degree, this is an exercise in repositioning yourself within the organization.

When you make an internal move, keep in mind that . . .

You Can't Control the Context

Although you may not be able to influence the circumstances surrounding an open role, you often can influence planned promotions and moves in advance.

Under a planned move, you will usually have time to do some due diligence and transition planning before you are officially named.

However, when a move is unplanned, you must figure out the real story before jumping into the new role. Don't be caught off guard by the surprise of the move and forget to do your required due diligence. For you to be successful it is important for you to have some level of understanding of the true backstory behind the unplanned move. The story may be a positive one or it may be ripe with controversy, but either way, you must know.

Finally, be sure to clarify and deliver expectations whether it is a permanent role or an interim appointment. Determining delivery expectations in a permanent role is an easier process, but interim roles can be tricky because delivery expectations can be all over the map and often contradictory. If an interim transition is to be successful there must be agreement across the key stakeholders on expected results and time frames.

It's Hard to Make a Clean Break

In many ways, you are in the new job at the moment of the announcement regardless of what may be announced as your official start date. Unlike coming in from the outside, people know you and can instantly start thinking or imagining you in that role. You may even start to get calls regarding issues and decisions related to the role. Even with these new demands coming at you before you've officially started, you are still accountable for results in your old job.

More often than not you will still be accountable for your old job even after you start your new job. Going back to the relay-runner analogy, you're really making two handoffs at the same time: the baton you're picking up from the person who had your new job before you and the baton you're handing off to the person taking your old job. With regard to your old job, you don't want to be in a position where you hand the baton over too quickly, too roughly, or not in the place it was requested.

If you falter with the transition of your old job, the results can impinge on your success in your new role. As you reset your stakeholder list for your new role, also keep in mind that you now have an extra set of stakeholders—those that helped you along the way. They will not want to see you flub the transition after helping position you for your new role.

There Is No Honeymoon

As an insider, you're expected to be fully up to speed the moment you start your new job. The good news is that you already have an internal network that you can begin to leverage immediately after your new role is announced. Although a promotion is certainly good news and lateral transfers may be as well, don't be blinded to the fact that in addition to your supporters, you'll most likely have detractors as well. You'll want to identify them early and keep them on your stakeholder list.

All this leads to three indicated actions for those promoted from within:

1. **Prepare in advance.** Work to understand the context and complexity of the new situation. Get yourself ready and exert whatever influence you can to shape your new role and set up success—as far in advance as possible.
2. **Take control of your own transition.** Be proactive and control the message and communication cascade—the timing of who hears what, in what order, in what medium—as well as clarifying what's changed and what has not changed. Protect your base by ensuring ongoing positive results in your old job and recognizing those who have helped you along the way.
3. **Accelerate team progress after the start.** This is where your knowledge of the organization can really help you. You and your new team can get a running start, leveraging positive momentum to accelerate the key strategic, operational, and organizational processes.

Prepare in Advance

The context of your move will impact the early leadership challenges you face. The smoothest and easiest transitions follow planned promotions or moves. When succession planning works and the right leader is in the right spot at the right time, most feel in control and few feel threatened. When this happens to you, be grateful and make the best of a good situation.

But it's not always like that. When there's a sudden leadership gap and you get an unexpected call to fill it like Gillian did, there's a significant challenge to regain control of the situation and of the rampant runaway emotions. Uncertainty and sudden change are scary for all.

Work to understand the thinking behind the decision and begin communicating with and understanding your new stakeholders. Beware of writing people off as stakeholders or influences too quickly, only to find that they really can have an impact on how your organization sees (and evaluates) you. Look carefully at the number and quality of things changing in your own situation. You'll need far more help if you're getting moved to run a new function in a new industry in a new country than if you're taking over from the boss whose deputy you've been for the last decade.

An internal promotion suggests that senior management sees value in continuity, insider knowledge, and a known entity (you) rather than the risk, hassle, and ramp-up time of an outsider. There may be an expectation of change, however, and insiders often lose grip of their opportunity by being afraid to rock the boat or by letting key collaborators assume that nothing's really going to change. Get a clear sense of the expectations and deliver accordingly.

Manage Right through the Interim

Perhaps the most challenging case is when you have to fill a gap as the interim leader. Get clarity on whether interim means "holding the fort until we find the right person, which absolutely will not be you," "on probation with a good chance of becoming permanent," or "doing the job as a developmental opportunity on the way to something else." In either case, it's likely a good posture to engage fully with the work itself while eschewing the perks of the job—basically, focusing your efforts on the least prestigious, highest impact tasks and leaving the glory to others.

Whatever the context, pause for a moment to craft a solid transition plan that includes the identification of key stakeholders and getting clear on your message. Then, get a head start before you start—jump-starting relationships with key stakeholders in particular.

Take Control of Your Own Transition

You will be perceived as starting your new job at the moment of the announcement, so try to control the timing of that announcement—particularly if you're moving into a vacant position. Remember that the announcement process includes far more than just the formal announcement itself. There are almost always leaks in advance and there are always people who should be told in advance, so you must be discerning about the cascade of information. In many cases you have to manage this down to a minute-by-minute level of detail to make sure that people hear about the promotion in the right order, in the right way, from the right person.

This is not a trivial issue. Be particularly sensitive to when, how, and from whom people hear.

Emotions will probably be running high and those hearing about the transition may include those who

- Are being moved out of a job
- Have allies or friends being moved out of a job
- See someone else is getting a role they might have wanted
- See this transition as particularly important to their own success— especially direct reports into and peers of the new role

If you're tempted to simply make one general and official announcement, think again. Trust and relationship building start with how people receive this kind of information. Anybody who gets a special advance notice will feel special, and as a first-time leader you want to use that capital wisely.

On the other hand, it's likely to be impossible for you to do all the one-on-one announcement meetings that you'd like. Even if you could, by the time you did your third or fourth, the others on your list probably would have already heard. Also, in many cases, you want to have somebody else relay the information, helping frame the message in the context of that person's specific role or reporting situation. It's worth thinking all this through and then designing a communication campaign that simply and effectively reaches your key stakeholders.

Start by understanding that there are no secrets. It's not so much that the people you trust with secrets intentionally pass them on, but that they inadvertently slip. An HR executive's secretary asked George how people always seemed to find out about promotions in advance.

> It's easy. A senior HR person walks into our general manager's office carrying their big personnel ring binder. People take a guess and then go to that HR executive's assistant and say "Great news about Larry. Isn't it?" Nine times out of 10, the HR assistant comes back with something along the lines of "It is." or "Larry? Don't you mean Doug?" Either way, they will figure it out.

You can't possibly anticipate and prevent all the different ways information is going to leak. Just assume it will and guide the cascade of leaks as much as you can.

"I'm here to listen" is an important part of any transition announcement. Knowing that your message is also an invitation for communication is critical to achieving a successful transition. The anxiety that change triggers can be greatly allayed by inclusive communication.

Announcement Cascade Time Line

Use the announcement cascade tool from Chapter 7 (Tool 7.14) as a guideline to craft your transition communication cascade. Let's walk through the key components of stakeholders, message, preannouncement, formal announcement, and post-announcement:

Stakeholders

Start with mapping and prioritizing the internal and external stakeholders who may be impacted by the transition.

Internal stakeholders might include

- Former peers who helped you and your team get to the point where you deserve this new move.
- New peers who are going to help you and your team be successful in advance.
- Other people in your informal network inside the company—no matter what their level or official role—who can help you or your team learn and get things done (perhaps including the incumbent under the right circumstances).
- Former and new team members.

External stakeholders might include

- Key customers—particularly those with close relationships with people involved in the changes.

- Key suppliers and analysts.
- Community leaders, government officials, regulators, and the like.

Message
The platforms for change, vision, and call to action in a transition situation aren't any different from those you'd use when coming in from the outside. The point is to clarify them before you do anything else.

Preannouncement Time Line
Map the order in which you're going to tell people in advance, understanding that the more people you tell, the further in advance, the greater the amount of leaks there will be.

Formal Announcement
This is the formal mass communication that goes out. Be clear on what it says, who says it, and exactly when it's distributed. This will influence your post-announcement time line.

Post-announcement Time Line
Now that the cat's out of the bag, you don't have to worry about leaks anymore, but you do need to control the order of the communications. You can do this by using a combination of mass, large-group, small-group, and one-on-one sessions to get your message out to the people you need to reach in a time frame that supports your announcement objectives.

"Presume Not That I Am the Thing I Was"[7]

After the announcement of your promotion or move, be as clear as possible about what's changed and what's the same. People are going to try to figure out the new you as quickly as they can. Everything you say and don't say, do and don't do will be interpreted and misinterpreted by someone—especially former peers who are now subordinates.

"Everyone" includes those staying behind in your old world. In some cases, you'll be asked to continue to manage your old role during the transition. In others, someone else will pick it up. But in all cases, the positive or negative results in your old job will impact people's perceptions of you. This is why you must protect your base, ideally by making sure that you've got someone ready to fill your old role and working with them to support a smooth transition. Their success is your success.

BRAVE TIP

Strive to shorten the time between announcement and start: one of the biggest differences between joining from the outside and getting moved from within is that more time between announcement and start is better when joining from the outside—to give you time for preparation and pre-boarding conversations. On the other hand, when moved from within, less time between announcement and start is better—to minimize the period when you're doing two jobs.

Accelerate Progress after the Start

Many leaders promoted from the inside underestimate how quickly the organization will change their perception about them and how quickly and naturally a new pecking order takes place. Most people are simply practical about this kind of change. "Well, Ron's the boss now. Let's figure out how he wants these things done and do it that way." Be aware, however, that not everybody is so pragmatic and accepting. Inside knowledge goes two ways. Your network includes supporters . . . and detractors. Some of those detractors are people you rubbed the wrong way in previous roles, others will be created during this transition. Watch out for those who wanted all or part of your new job and be prepared for some people to work against your success. As Sun-Tzu says, "Keep your friends close, and your enemies closer."[8]

Some of this is, perhaps, inevitable. Make sure that you've got your supporters, scouts, and seconds keeping you aware of the mood of the larger group and what any detractors might be doing or saying. You should try to counter negativity as much as practical. This is important, but don't get overinvested in this.

When Gillian started her role within her family's business, she was not well received by everyone, and she could feel it. It was hard for her not to get wrapped up in it, and she realized quickly that she couldn't control people's perceptions of her; all she could do was be positive, professional, and most importantly, herself. If some people don't turn around, then you may not want them on your team. Your goal is to create positive momentum quickly, and then turn your attention to accelerating progress by evolving the people, plans, and practices.

Adjusting to a New Boss[9]

Sometimes in interim roles, you'll have an overlap with the person replacing you at the back end. Even though that's a relatively short period inside an interim assignment, take it seriously. It doesn't matter how successful you and your team have been. It doesn't matter what your previous results and ratings were. Whether it's interim or permanent, a new boss reshuffles the deck, just as you do when you're the new boss.

Given that, here are some tips for adjusting to a new boss under any circumstances:

Foundation. Treat your new boss decently as a human being; make the boss feel welcome, valued, and valuable. Enable the new boss to do good work. Do your job well—and not the boss's.

Attitude. Choose to be optimistic. Believe the best about your new boss. Focus on these positives at all times with all people, making sure that your spouse and closest confidants do the same. Avoid unguarded carping.

Approach. Proactively tell your new boss that you want to be part of the new team and follow up with actions that reinforce this.

Learning. Present a realistic and honest game plan to help the boss learn. This will likely pay important dividends.

Clarify the situation and plans, offering objective options.

Seek out the new boss's perspective early and often and be open to new directions.

Expectations. Understand and move on your new boss's agenda immediately. Know the boss's priorities.

Know what the new boss thinks your priorities should be.

Decide what resources you both agree to invest in your area.

Implementation. Adjust to your new boss's working style immediately. This is a hard shift, not an evolution.

Control points: Give the boss requested information, in the format desired, at the frequency wanted.

Decisions: Clarify decision-making choices (when each of you decides; when each of you provides input). Remember, the old rules are out. It's a new game.

Communication: Clarify the boss's preferred mode, manner, frequency, and how disagreements are managed.

Readjust your team's imperative, if necessary, to match your new boss's vision.

Delivery. Be on your A game.

Be present and "on"—everything done by you and your team will be part of your new boss's evaluation of you.

Deliver early wins that are important to your new boss and to the people he or she listens to. (In a restart, the score is reset. Your old wins and your team's old wins are history.)

You Deserve It

Perhaps the most important thing to keep in mind is that you got the promotion or move because key people were confident that you would be successful.

Those key people together probably know more about the situation than you do. Furthermore, because you're getting promoted or moved from within, they know you. To paraphrase Virgil, if those key people think you can and you think you can, you certainly can. So, prepare in advance as much as you can. Take control of your own transition as much as you can and accelerate team progress after the start as much as you can. If you can manage that, then you and your teams can successfully transition the batons and do great things.

SUMMARY: TAKE CHARGE OF YOUR NEW TEAM

In all cases,

- Get a head start by having a plan and jump-starting relationships.
- Manage the message by making sure what you do matches what you say matches what you fundamentally believe.
- Build the team by applying the components of BRAVE leadership.

When getting promoted from within,

- Prepare in advance, especially around securing the resources and support you'll need going forward.
- Take control of your own transition, especially around deciding what to keep the same and what to change.
- Accelerate team progress after your start by evolving the strategies first, and then operations and organization.

Chapter 3

THE BRAVE LEADERSHIP SUCCESS FRAMEWORK: BEHAVIORS, RELATIONSHIPS, ATTITUDE, VALUES, ENVIRONMENT

The components of BRAVE leadership include behaviors, relationships, attitude, values, and environment.

- Behaviors are the actions that make real, lasting impact on others.
- Relationships are the heart of leadership. If you can't connect, you can't lead.
- Attitude is often the pivot point for clarifying how the team is going to win.
- Values are the bedrock of a high-performing team. Get clear on what really matters and why.
- Environment sets the context for everything else. Know where you are playing.

BEHAVIORS: HOW YOU GET THINGS DONE THROUGH OTHER PEOPLE

Do not confuse motion and progress. A rocking horse keeps moving but does not make any progress.

—Alfred A. Montapert

Don't mistake activity with achievement.

—John Wooden

Am I inventing things to do to avoid the important?
—Timothy Ferris, *The 4-Hour Workweek*

There are no prizes for effort after the fifth grade. The key is to focus on those very few things that will lead to forward progress and achievement—impact. These are the things that create the greatest value for your team's internal and external customers.

RELATIONSHIPS: THE HEART OF LEADERSHIP

You can't lead anyone unless you can connect with them. Connecting requires communication. And everything you do and don't do, say and don't say, listen to or observe and ignore, communicates. Make conscious choices. Get clear on your message. Drive that through your words and actions. This is the heart of leadership and a mandatory component of inspiring and enabling others as a first-time leader.

ATTITUDE: MAKE CRUCIAL CHOICES AROUND YOUR TEAM'S STRATEGY, POSTURE, AND CULTURE

Attitude is the pivot point between environment and values on the one side and relationships and behaviors on the other side. Strategies are step down. One level's strategies become the next level's objectives. If the level up from you has a strategy of growing in Brazil and Russia and you're in charge of Brazil, growth is your objective. The question for you is how to grow, your strategy. Then, armed with your strategic choices, make sure your posture and culture line up with them.

VALUES: ALIGN YOURSELF AND YOUR TEAM WITH THE ORGANIZATION'S MISSION, VISION, AND VALUES— MORE OR LESS

What we're calling values has two parts: your mission and vision, and your principles. Mission is generally given to you. You don't have a choice. Vision is your picture of success. Principles are the things you will not compromise on the way to delivering that mission and achieving that vision. Together, they comprise purpose.

ENVIRONMENT: GET CLEAR ON YOUR MISSION AND FIELDS OF ACTION

Context matters. Part of your team's context is made up of the choices the broader organization has made. If you've been assigned a particular sandbox, play in that sandbox. Part of your context is made up of the rest of the world. Understanding the context is a critical piece of framing your decisions.

BUILDING UP THE BRAVE LEADERSHIP FRAMEWORK FROM THE OUTSIDE IN

Behaviors flow from relationships—the heart of leadership. But you can't get there until you're aligned on the environment, values, and attitude choices. Thus, we suggest building up your BRAVE leadership framework from the outside in, from the environment, through values and attitudes, to relationships and behaviors.

Part II

BUILD YOUR BRAVE LEADERSHIP FROM THE OUTSIDE IN

Chapter 4

ENVIRONMENT: GET CLEAR ON YOUR MISSION AND FIELDS OF ACTION

First-time leaders often react to their new situations by asking, "What have I gotten myself into?" The good news is that that is exactly the right question. As Steven Covey put it, "Seek first to understand."[1] Seek to understand the context for your leadership and then make choices around where to focus with that context in mind. This will make things in the future much more straightforward.

For Zappos CEO Tony Hsieh, the most important decision is where to play. He learned that playing poker. He applied it at Zappos. In Hsieh's words,

> Through reading poker books and practicing by playing, I spent a lot of time learning about the best strategy to play once I was actually sitting down at a table. My big "ah-ha!" moment came when I finally learned that the game started even before I sat down in a seat.
>
> In a poker room at a casino, there are usually many different choices of tables. Each table has different stakes, different players, and different dynamics that change as the players come and go, and as players get excited, upset, or tired.
>
> I learned that the most important decision I could make was which table to sit at.[2]

We suggest thinking about this in three steps: What? So what? Now what?

1. Understand the business environment, organizational history, recent results (what)
2. Align around an interpretation of the situation assessment (so what)
3. Make clear choices around where to play and where not to play (now what)

UNDERSTAND CONTEXT

The context for your leadership is made up of the business environment, organizational history, and recent results.

Business Environment: 5Cs Situation Assessment

As a first-time leader, you'll find it helpful to have some frameworks for your thinking. (And we did promise we'd give you frameworks and tools.) The 5Cs Situation Assessment is a framework for understanding the business environment by looking at customers, collaborators, capabilities, competitors, and conditions:

Customers: First line, customer chain, end users, influencers.
Collaborators: Suppliers, allies, government/community leaders.
Capabilities: Human, operational, financial, technical, key assets.
Competitors: Direct, indirect, potential.
Conditions: Social/demographic, political/government/regulatory, economic, market.

While there will be other things you need to look at, this will give you a good start.

Customers

Customers include the people your organization sells to or serves. This includes direct customers who actually give you money. It also includes their customers, their customers' customers, and so on down the line. Eventually, there are end users or consumers of whatever the output of that chain is. Additionally, there are the people who influence your various customers' purchase decisions. Take all of these into account.

Federal Express sells overnight delivery services to corporate purchasing departments that contract those services on behalf of business managers. But the real decision makers are those managers' administrative assistants. So, Federal Express targets its marketing efforts not at the people who write the checks, not at the managers, but at the core influencers. They aim advertising and media at those influencers and have their drivers pick the packages up from the administrative assistants personally instead of going through an impersonal mailroom.

Collaborators

Collaborators include your suppliers, business allies, and people delivering complementary products and services. What links all these groups together is that they will do better if you do better. So it's in their best interest, whether they know it or not, to help you succeed. Think Microsoft and Intel. Think hot dogs and mustard.

Just as these relationships are two-way, so must be your analysis. You need to understand the interdependencies and reciprocal commitments. Whenever these dependencies and commitments are out of balance, the nature of the relationships will inevitably change.

Think through your customer's purchasing cycle. Who comes before you? Who comes after you? If you're in corporate real estate, a relocation expert you can vouch for and trust is an obvious ally. However, a printing business could be your ally, as your customers will need new letterhead and business cards to reflect their new location. Collaborators are strategic partnerships, so think strategically.

Capabilities

Capabilities are those abilities that can help you deliver a differentiated, better product or service to your customers. These abilities include everything from access to materials and capital to plants and equipment to people to patents. Pay particular attention to people, plans, and practices.

Competitors

Competitors are those whom your customers could give their money or attention to instead of to you. It is important to take a wide view of potential competitors. Amtrak's real competitors are other forms of transportation like automobiles and airplanes. The competition for consumer dollars may be as varied as a child's college education versus a Disney World vacation. In analyzing these competitors, it is important to think through their objectives, strategies, and situation, as well as strengths and weaknesses, to better understand and predict what they might do next.

Conditions

Conditions are a catchall for everything going on in the environment in which you do business. At a minimum, look at social and political, demographic, and economic trends and determine how those trends might impact the organization over the short-, mid-, and long-term.

Macro elements:
- Demographic
- Economic
- Political/government/ regulatory
- Technology
- Market

TOOL 4.1
5Cs SITUATION ANALYSIS GUIDELINES

1. Customers (first line, customer chain, end users, influencers) Needs, hopes, preferences, commitments, strategies, price/value perspectives by segment.

First line/direct customers
- Universe of opportunity—total market, volume by segment
- Current situation—volume by customer, profit by customer

Customer chain
- Customers' customers—total market, volume by segment
- Current customers' strategies, volume, and profitability by segment

End users
- Preference, consumption, usage, loyalty, and price value data and perceptions for our products and competitors' products

Influencers
- Key influencers of customer and end user purchase and usage decisions

2. Collaborators (suppliers, business allies, partners, government/community leaders)

- Strategies, profit/value models for external and internal stakeholders (up, across, down).

3. Capabilities
- Human (includes style and quality of management, strategy dissemination, culture)
- Operational (includes integrity of business processes, effectiveness of organization structure, links between measures and rewards and corporate governance)
- Financial (includes capital and asset utilization and investor management)
- Technical (includes core processes, IT systems, supporting skills)
- Key assets (includes brands and intellectual property)

4. Competitors (Direct, indirect, potential)

- Strategies, profit/value models, profit pools by segment, source of pride.

5. Conditions

Social/demographic—trends
Political/government/regulatory—trends
Economic—macro and micro—trends
Market definition, inflows, outflows, substitutes—trends

Pulling it together:

SWOT analysis and thinking about:

- Sources, drivers, hinderers of revenue, and value
- Current strategy/resource deployment: Coherent? Adequate? De facto strategy?
- Insights and scenarios (To set up: What?/So what?/Now what?)

Copyright © PrimeGenesis® LLC. To customize this document, download Tool 4.1 from the First-Time Leader page on www.onboardingtools.com.

Organizational History

If you see a static picture of a pencil on a table you can only guess in which direction the pencil is rolling. If you see part of a video of a pencil rolling across a table, the direction of its roll is readily apparent. The same is true with an organization. Knowing how it started and developed are valuable inputs into understanding its direction.

Hewlett Packard began in a garage. It developed as a family company, seeped in the founder's values and "way." A couple of recent CEOs of Hewlett Packard ignored that history and tried to move the organization forward in ways that simply did not work. Don't do that. Understand the history.

Yearley/Toll Example[3]

Put yourself in Doug Yearley's shoes in November 2009. You've just been named EVP on the way to becoming CEO of luxury homebuilder Toll Brothers, a company that lost $750 million in the year that just ended due to accounting write downs. You're entering the fifth year of a recession in your industry. Your core revenues were down 44 percent versus the prior year, and 75 percent versus the peak a few years before. If there was ever an organization that required significant change, this was it. Right?

Wrong.

Yearley had to engage this culture and his colleagues in the right context. Doug knew three things as he transitioned into his role as the second CEO ever at the company:

1. The organization was strong. It had cash in the bank and solid processes in place, including a long-standing management review every Monday evening.
2. He was an integral part of that organization. Yearley had been there for 20 years and steadily progressed as a leader. At the point he took over from Robert Toll as CEO in June 2010, he had spent 800 Monday evenings with Robert on those management calls.
3. He knew what he could control and what he could not control, and he was confident that Toll would come through the dark days and emerge stronger.

Two years later, it looked like they were weathering the storm. Even though the housing market was still bleak, Toll had just announced its fifth straight quarterly profits. As Yearley was quick to point out, not enough profits—but they were profits. They had $4.2 billion cash and $800 million in available credit.

Yearley, Robert Toll, and their team did a couple of things right.

Face the Brutal Truths Head On

First, they faced the brutal truths head on. As Yearley explained to George, "This incredibly deep and dark housing recession is like none we've ever seen before." They were continually "right sizing" where they had to, centralizing purchasing and watching incentives. They were managing cash carefully. Delivering even small profits with revenues down 75 percent is no mean trick.

Position Yourself for Future Success

Second, they were positioning themselves to take advantage of the upturn when it comes. As Yearley told George,

> Because we have a strong cash position and balance sheet . . . I can challenge the company to look into new ideas. . . . This keeps it exciting for people even though sales may not be where we want them to be.

Those new ideas included

- Continuing their push into urban (started in 2003—22 percent of their revenues now come from high-rises in New York City)
- Looking at international opportunities
- Establishing Gibraltar Capital to buy distressed portfolios of loans
- Looking at new markets within the United States

What Yearley did not do was panic. He did not shock the system. He was confident that he and his team could continue to right size the company, grow, and return to meaningful profitability.

Implications for you: Understand the context. It may change your mind about what to do.

Understand as much as you can about the spark that created the organization, the founders, and the early starter team—how it developed, its stories and myths. They are all real—in at least some members' minds. Do this on a macro level for the entire organization. Do this on a micro level for whatever team you are called to lead. Do this on a personal level for the most important individual members of the team so you understand their individual stories.

Recent Results

The third piece of context, in addition to business environment and organizational history, is recent results. Surprise, surprise! An organization that has been performing well and meeting its goals is going to be less open to change than one that has been missing targets. The level of confidence of team members used to winning will be different from those who have had setbacks.

Similar to history, look at recent results on organizational, team, and individual levels.

ALIGN AROUND AN INTERPRETATION OF THE SITUATION ASSESSMENT

Leadership is about inspiring and enabling others. Understanding the context for your leadership is necessary, but not sufficient. You're not done until your team is aligned around an interpretation of that context. Of course individual team members will have their own different perspectives. This is not about getting to 100 percent congruence. It is about getting to a consensus around the most important elements, how people feel about them—so what?

SWOT

A SWOT (internal Strengths and Weaknesses versus external Opportunities and Threats) analysis is a good way to drive to consensus around strengths, weaknesses, opportunities, threats, key leverage points, business issues, and sustainable competitive advantages.

Strengths are resources and capabilities that give the organization advantages.

Weaknesses are gaps in resources and capabilities that make the organization vulnerable.

Opportunities are things happening in the world outside the organization that should make it easier for the organization to succeed. People often get this wrong, putting in ideas here around what the organization might do. Don't do that yet. Follow the process and keep this section focused on things happening outside the organization.

Threats are things happening in the world outside the organization that make it more difficult for the organization to sustain or succeed. Remember to keep this focused on external threats.

Key leverage points are the internal strengths that can be brought to bear to take advantage of external opportunities. These are the corridors of ways to win. For example, if you have a strong beverage distribution system and the public water supply is contaminated, you could leverage your system to deliver safe bottled water to people. This is the first of the So what? thinking sections.

Business issues are the areas of internal weakness that are particularly vulnerable to external threats. Fixing these is a way to avoid losing. If you have only marginally acceptable safety standards in your plants and there is pending legislation to increase legal safety standards well beyond those that you currently meet, that is a potential issue. This is the second of the So what? thinking sections.

Finally, the *sustainable competitive advantage* is most likely one of the key leverage points that can be sustained in the face of business issues.

SWOT is an extremely valuable tool. You'll find yourself using it over and over again. Gillian has often used it as a team exercise, as it gets everyone on board aligned with vision and strategy and starting to think in terms of So what?

Another valuable tool gets at where value is created—Gadiesh and Gilber's Profit Pools tool. On the one hand, it's deceptively simple. Map revenue on the horizontal axis and operating margin on the vertical axis. Out pops a graphic showing you the relative size of the profit pools. On the other hand, it tends to reveal some surprising things. For example, in the 1980s, a surprisingly large portion of the auto industry's profits was in car financing.

Complete the SWOT analysis.

Use it (and profit pools where appropriate) to help you understand the sources, drivers, hinderers of revenue, and value.

Take a look at the current strategy/resource deployment: Coherent? Adequate? De facto strategy?

Think through your insights and potential scenarios (to complete So what? and set up Now what? choices).

TOOL 4.2
SWOT

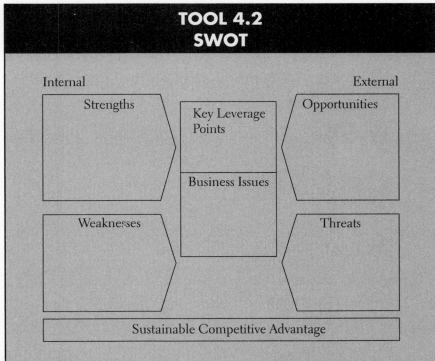

Internal   External

Strengths

Key Leverage Points

Opportunities

Business Issues

Weaknesses

Threats

Sustainable Competitive Advantage

Strengths	Internal to organization—things we do better
Weaknesses	Internal to organization—things we do worse
Opportunities	External to organization—things to capitalize on
Threats	External to organization—things to worry about

Key Leverage Points

Opportunities we can leverage our strengths against (where to play to win)

Business Implications

Threats our weaknesses make us vulnerable to (where to play not to lose)

Sustainable Competitive Advantages

Key leverage points that can be sustained over extended period of time

TOOL 4.3
PROFIT POOLS

Operating Margin		
100%		
90%		
80%		
70%		
60%		
50%		
40%		
30%		
20%		
10%		
0%		
	Share of Industry Revenue	**100%**

To customize this document, download Tool 4.3 from the First-Time Leader page on www.onboardingtools.com.

MAKE CLEAR CHOICES AROUND WHERE TO PLAY AND WHERE NOT TO PLAY

With the first two parts complete, you're now ready to make your choices around where to play and where not to play.

Play to your strengths. We've learned this over and over again. It's far more productive to build on your strengths than to correct your weaknesses. Adding 10 percent to your business where you have a large market share is almost always easier and more valuable than adding 10 percent where you have a small share.

Chalef/KnowledgeTree Example

Where to play is generally the first of the five core questions a BRAVE leader needs to answer. In theory, this is done by solving someone's problem after choosing which customers to serve and which of their problems to solve. Industries and competitors, business models, places in the value chain, and geography all play a role in the selection leaders make.

But as infamous computer scientist Jan L. A. Van De Snepscheut noted, "In theory, there is no difference between theory and practice. But in practice, there is." Just ask KnowledgeTree's CEO Daniel Chalef.

Which Problem to Solve

Founded as a systems integrator, KnowledgeTree soon understood its customers needed document management. So Chalef and his team built an open source document manager, which worked so well that increasingly more people found it and used it over time. Soon, KnowledgeTree's core business morphed. As Chalef told George, "The market found us as opposed to us looking for a problem to solve."

Which Business Model

KnowledgeTree's business model continues to evolve. Having moved into the document management business, it realized the future was in the cloud and changed from helping people manage documents behind the firewall to helping them manage documents in the cloud. Then it realized that just managing documents wasn't enough and built tools and skills to curate, use, and draw insights from documents to solve "higher order problems."

Value Chain Focal Point

Similarly, KnowledgeTree's value chain focus has changed. Chalef suggests all start-ups need to be ready to change. "In a start-up, it's dynamic." In KnowledgeTree's case, it began with design and is now focused on delivery. Chalef suspects they'll need to build out more and more support capabilities as they work with ever-larger customers.

Geography

For many, there's a geographical dimension to the where to play question. Michael Porter et al. have made a strong case for the power of geographically clustered industry hubs like film in Hollywood and Bollywood and fashion design in Milan.

Chalef started KnowledgeTree in South Africa. As it expanded, he looked for the optimal place to locate his business. He was initially attracted to Silicon Valley but quickly realized the time-zone difference with South Africa was too challenging, so he contemplated Boston. Unfortunately, the South African native wasn't in favor of winter weather. Enter Raleigh, North Carolina, which offered a technology cluster in a time zone closer to his South African developers and a more moderate climate.

Where to Play in Practice

Where to play choices:

- Which problem to solve (for which customers)?
- Which business model?
- Value chain focal point?
- Geography?

Don't get us wrong. Having a framework is important. Customers and their problems, your business model, value chain, and geographic choices are important. Just don't follow the theory off the cliff. Theoretically elegant has no value if it's not practically useful. Chalef says he made his decisions partly with scientific methods and partly with gut feel. Not a bad way to approach getting the best of theory and practice.[4]

Implications for you: Take into account the theoretical, but drive to the practical.

Nike used an interesting approach in its expansion, changing only one variable at a time. For example, their first entry into any international market was with running shoes branded Nike.

Sport:	running	=>	new sport	or	running	or	running	or	running
Item:	shoes		shoes		**shorts**		shoes		shoes
Brand:	Nike		Nike		Nike		**new brand**		Nike
Geography:	USA		USA		USA		USA		**new country**

Ideally, you can find ways to leverage your strengths against new and emerging opportunities. Ideally, you can find ways to do this requiring you to change as few variables as possible.

Of course you have to do some work to shore up your areas of vulnerability. If your boat has a hole in it, you might sink if you don't fix it. But fixing the hole won't win you the race. It will just keep you from losing.

Patrick/Proxima and Carticept Example

"Where it matters and where you can win" is the answer to the first of the five most important questions for BRAVE leaders: Where to play?

George's wife and he had a mantra when their children were little. They only confronted the kids when (a) it mattered and (b) they could win. What mattered tended to be things making material differences to the children's well-being or putting themselves or others at risk. Generally, they could win things that did not violate basic laws of nature. (For example, trying to get a two-week-old to sleep through the night was a nonstarter.)

This framework works for organizations as well. Choose to play where it matters and where you can win.

Look at this from several different levels, taking into account the macro environment, your organization's place in the macro environment, and your place in your organization. Across those levels, what matters are generally things aligned with meaningful and rewarding shared purposes. Where you can win generally involves some sort of sustainable competitive advantage that doesn't defy the laws of nature.

Tim Patrick has done this twice: at Proxima and at Carticept.

Proxima

When researchers at Johns Hopkins developed a unique way of radiating cancer allowing quicker and more efficient treatment, Patrick saw this as a partnership opportunity. Together, they used this technology on brain cancers with positive results. Patrick also realized he could take that technology and apply it to other cancers. While there were 20,000 incidents of brain cancer in the United States, there were 200,000 incidents of breast cancer. So, Patrick built Proxima to play in that space, solving an unmet clinical need, making a positive impact on patients, and generating a good financial return. It mattered. They could win.

Carticept

Having sold Proxima, Patrick next looked at the aging population and the more than 40 million people in the United States who suffer or will suffer from some form of arthritis. Many of them will need joint replacements. That matters to a lot of people. But Patrick realized he couldn't win there. Why? The big orthopedic companies were well established in the space.

The unmet clinical need was in the area of steroid injections. Other than the publicity surrounding some sports heroes (and fallen heroes), this area was getting relatively little attention. Enter Carticept's portable ultrasound-guided injections, dramatically improving the accuracy of local applications of steroids to local injuries. Once again, Patrick had identified an unmet clinical need that mattered and where his organization could win.

But the world has changed. It's tougher and takes longer to get FDA (Food and Drug Administration) approvals than it did when Patrick was building Proxima. At Proxima, Patrick sprinted. He created a culture of risk takers to build the business fast and sell it. At Carticept, Patrick is running a marathon. So he's built a different culture and formed a strategic partnership with SonoSite to cross-distribute products and generate revenues to fund the extra time he needs to get his approvals. He's playing where it matters and where he can win, just differently.

Where It Matters and Where You Can Win

Where it matters is most likely going to be where there is an unmet need that has a meaningful impact on people's lives. Where you can win is not just where you have strengths, but where you have differentiated strengths from others playing in or around your space.[5]

Implications for you: There is no value in sameness. Be different.

The Now what? of where to play is to take the So what? consensus alignment around your What? context and make choices around where to play—and not play.

George once asked one of his bosses to help prioritize 10 tasks he was working on. His boss said they were all top priority. George replied that that meant they were all the same and therefore average. For something to be top priority, something else must be lower priority.

Remember that when delegating tasks to your team.

Hussain/Imprivata Example

Choosing where to play is the CEO's big bet. He or she must lead the strategic direction of the company by examining the business environment, organizational history, and recent results.

It's essential to get clear on the organization's purpose and principles, attitude and values that will have the most meaningful impact. But all those considerations follow the first question, Where to play?

Omar Hussain took the bet.

Imprivata's Gamble

Hussain is CEO of Imprivata, which started as a single sign-on provider and transformed into a health care IT security company. Imprivata was a successful start-up that grew to $20 million in revenue in five years. Approximately 60 percent of that revenue came from health care and 40 percent from other industries. As Hussain explained to George, he realized they could not "build the business without building the value." His owners were venture capitalists, who lived by the mantra "Go big or go home."

Hussain decided that Imprivata needed to solve fewer, bigger problems. The real opportunity was in health care IT security—a big problem that no one was solving. "When we took a step back it was clear there were external market conditions were driving rapid growth in our healthcare business," said Hussain.

The industry was in the middle of a dramatic transformation from paper to electronic health records (EHRs). The security and privacy regulations that accompanied that shift made it arduous for doctors to access information, without disrupting or slowing patient care. This made doctors reluctant to adopt the new systems because it was easier to open a paper chart than to log in and out of several clinical applications, dozens of times a day.

Hussain's wanted to fix that. "Our technology eased that burden and enabled fast, secure access to electronic patient information making it easier for doctors to adopt EHR systems to help organizations meet Meaningful Use objectives," said Hussain. Secure single sign-on technology in health care is a big market in a multitrillion dollar industry and a "hill [they] could own."

Most people tend to invest a little in new ideas, getting there step-by-step. Hussain didn't think that would work. He wanted to go all in.

Start with the DNA

Hussain felt good about Imprivata's DNA. It had "passionate people" with the "courage of their convictions" and the "creativity" to invent new solutions. "You are only as good as your people," he said.

Bring the Investors on Board

Hussain describes his investors as "strong, seasoned and mature." He told George that bringing them on board was the easiest step. Not surprising, since venture capitalists are in the business of making multiple bets.

Take the Bet

This was the big moment. There wasn't any sense of "Let's see how this plays out." No keeping half the resources in his pocket just in case. He didn't give his team a choice. As he puts it, "Leadership means you have to lead." It's easy to say and hard to do. As Hussain phrased it, "Once you say it, you must do it." And they did.

He "noticed the trend, read the tea leaves, and took the bet."

Leaders must make the choice about where to play—then follow through and drop the other shoe of where *not* to play. Make the decision. Take the bet. And then make sure everyone else understands the logic of the choice and follows through to make it happen. Play the card. Burn the bridges. Move forward.[6]

Implications for you: Choose where to play and where not to play. And make it clear.

Choosing where to play is necessary, but not sufficient. You must also choose where not to play. Choose to

- **Maintain** in less attractive areas where you have a competitive advantage.
- **Invest** in more attractive areas where you have a competitive advantage.
- **Build** advantages in more attractive areas where you do not have a competitive advantage.
- **Avoid** less attractive areas where you do not have a competitive advantage.

TOOL 4.4
WHERE TO PLAY CHOICES

	Maintain	Invest
Areas where we have competitive advantages		
	Not now, not ever	Build advantages for later
Areas where we do not have competitive advantages		
	Less attractive areas	More attractive areas

Copyright © PrimeGenesis® LLC. To customize this document, download Tool 4.4 from the First-Time Leader page on www.onboardingtools.com.

SUMMARY: WHERE TO PLAY

One of the most important choices you and your team make is where to play. You must understand the context in which you're operating and interpret and create context for others. Today's environment is highly charged in exciting and dangerous ways. So be sure to consider all the risks and opportunities both outside and inside your field of endeavor and organization.

- Understand the business environment, organizational history, recent results.
- Align around an interpretation of the situation assessment.
- Make clear choices around where to play and where not to play.
- Don't try to be everything to everyone.

Chapter 5

VALUES: ALIGN YOURSELF AND YOUR TEAM WITH THE ORGANIZATION'S MISSION, VISION, AND VALUES—MORE OR LESS

Leadership is about inspiring and enabling others to do their absolute best together to realize a meaningful and rewarding shared purpose. What matters is that shared purpose.

Virtually every experienced leader that has spoken at CEO Connection CEO Boot Camps has said that the number one job of any leader is to own the vision and values. It's true for experienced CEOs. It's true for first-time leaders. It's true for everyone in between. Get clear on your purpose—your mission, vision, and values.

Simon Sinek put it particularly well in his September 2009 TED talk in which he explained his "golden circle" of communicating from the *why* out instead of the *what* in.

It is remarkable and powerful when a leader gets it right. Nick Sarillo of Nick's Pizza & Pub, an Illinois-based family dining business, shared his ideas with George:

> The overriding message, I think, is that business leaders must explicitly define their organization's purpose. Defining our purpose first is critical because it shapes every other aspect of "BRAVE Leadership." Your organization's purpose shapes behaviors, relationships, attitudes and the work environment. The purpose, "why" we do what we do, creates a meaningful place to work. The values are also important in creating an intentional culture because they are "how" we do the "what," whether it is pizza or widgets or accounting.[1]

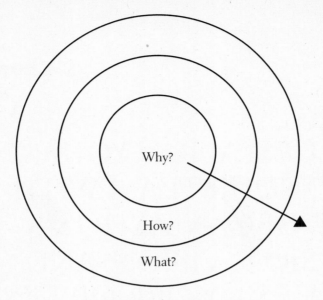

Golden Circle of Communicating

Why? How? What? This little idea explains why some organizations and some leaders are able to inspire where others aren't.
 And by "why" I don't mean "to make a profit." That's a result.
 By "why" I mean: what's your purpose? What's your cause? What's your belief?
 Why does your organization exist? Why do you get out of bed in the morning?
 And why should anyone care?
 People don't buy what you do; they buy why you do it.

Let's start with some definitions. Different people use these words in different ways. On the one hand, whatever works for you and your team is fine. On the other hand, for the purpose of this book, it's going to be easier if we all agree on one set of definitions. And since we're the ones doing the writing, your choice is either to accept our definitions or be confused.

> **Mission:** Why we are here, why we exist, what business we are in.
> **Vision:** Future picture—what we want to become, where we are going.
> **Values:** Beliefs and moral principles that guide attitudes, relationships, and behaviors.

It's useful to deal with these in the context of purpose and happiness.

THE SECRET OF HAPPINESS

Happiness is good. Actually, there are three goods. Everyone strives for each of the three though each person weights them differently. (Some weight them very differently.) The three goods are

1. Good for me
   - Near term pleasure (enjoyable work/activities, fit with life interests)
   - Compensation (monetary, nonmonetary reward, recognition, respect)
2. Good for others
   - Meaning in the work (impact on others, match with values)
   - Share in shaping the destiny (influence, being informed)
3. Good at it
   - Match of activities with strengths and resources (support and time)
   - Employability (learning, development, resume builder)

LINK BETWEEN HAPPINESS AND PURPOSE

As we've said, leadership is about inspiring and enabling others to do their absolute best together to realize a meaningful and rewarding shared purpose.

Now we're suggesting that happiness is good: good for others; good for me; good at it.

Cross the two:

Meaningful is about good for others.
Rewarding is about good for me.
Do their absolute best is doing what people are good at.

Or, leadership is about inspiring and enabling others to do their absolute best together (good at it) to realize a meaningful (good for others) and rewarding (good for me) shared purpose. Happiness matters.

MISSION

Mission: Why we are here, why we exist, what business we are in.

Your mission is about beliefs. The most inspiring leaders have a passion for what they do. This cannot be replicated or forced. It comes out of their pores, and others are attracted to that. People want to buy from people like this and work with people like this because they can see how much these people believe. BRAVE leaders flow their passion to the team so that everyone believes. BRAVE leaders won't stay in a position if they are not passionate and recognize when it's time to move on.

While some mission statements can be flat, those with a strong belief behind them stand out.

Simply put, a mission statement informs the organization of why it exists, what it is called to accomplish. The best mission statements are concise, clear, and motivating. They leave no question as to the higher good, good for others, or the ultimate focus of the organization. Your team should be able to apply the mission statement to everything they do. It should be so clear that they can relate it to any task.

The most common mistake that organizations make when crafting mission statements is making them so complex and convoluted that they fail to provide meaning for anyone. Keep them pointed, accurate, and inspiring. A few great mission statements:

> *Provide relief to victims of disasters and help people prevent, prepare for, and respond to emergencies.*
>
> —American Red Cross

> *Preserve and improve human life.*
>
> —Merck

> *To explore new worlds, discover new civilizations; seek out new life forms, and to boldly go where no one has gone before.*
>
> —Starship Enterprise

We don't know about you, but we find these much more inspiring than

To increase shareholder value
To be the most respected and admired market leader
To meet our customers' needs

Mission Tool

Mission development is a journey of discovery versus creation. Your mission is dictated by others' needs. Often it's handed to you. Other times you are called to it. Once you've made the choices around where to play and who to serve, the questions to ask are what do they need and why, and what must you deliver to meet those needs. Your mission flows from those.

TOOL 5.1
MISSION

Who needs us?

What do they need and why?

What must we deliver to meet their needs?

Thus, our mission:

Copyright © PrimeGenesis® LLC. To customize this document, download Tool 5.1 from the First-Time Leader page on www.onboardingtools.com.

Note: Get this right. It's going to inform everything else you do. If you and your boss and your team are not clear on your mission, stop and get clear. Do not even try to do anything else until you are clear on why you are doing what you are doing.

VISION

Vision: Future picture—what we want to become, where we are going.

A good vision is an appealing picture of future success, showing what things will be like when the mission is accomplished. Some examples of clear and inspiring visions:

The world's premier engineering organization. Trained and ready to provide support anytime, anyplace.
— U.S. Army Corps of Engineers

Create a world renowned, yet personable, showcase of maverick films, film-makers, and the technology that enables creativity.
— Cinequest

A world in which every child, everywhere, has equal access to life-saving vaccines.
— The Vaccine Fund

Critical point: the people the vision is designed to inspire must be able to picture themselves in the vision. Inspired members of the U.S. Army Corps of Engineers can see themselves trained and ready to provide support as part of the world's premier engineering organization. Inspired members of Cinequest can see themselves as part of a world renowned, yet personable showcase that enables creativity. Members of the Vaccine Fund can see themselves in a world in which every child, everywhere, has equal access to life-saving vaccines. These are rewarding pictures for these members.

TOOL 5.2
VISION

What will it look like when we achieve our mission?

Copyright © PrimeGenesis® LLC. To customize this document, download Tool 5.2 from the First-Time Leader page on www.onboardingtools.com.

Dreaming

One of Sinek's closing points in his TED talk was that Martin Luther King Jr.'s great Washington talk was not the "I have a plan" talk. It was the "I have a dream" talk. A vision is a dream.

Gillian does an exercise with her team once a year to plan out five-year goals. She encourages them to dream *big* (many are afraid to do that). She covers all aspects—Where will the company be? Who will our clients be? What roles will you have? What kinds of technologies will we be using? She makes sure they are as specific as possible. The first time she did this, some people thought she was crazy, but as the months went on and the team started ticking off some of the goals of year three in year one, they really got excited. They believed. Don't be afraid to dream—you never know where it can take you.

Carving out a vision with your team gets everyone on the same page. It comes from the team, not top down—which can be deflating. This is a critical component of inspiring others.

Often dreams from the top are very exciting and well intentioned, but there is a critical flaw—they don't align with middle management goals. Ensure that the vision is being supported at all levels of business.

VALUES

Values: Beliefs and moral principles that guide attitudes, relationships, and behaviors.

If you choose to have a values-driven organization, the end does not justify the means.

For these organizations, values are the bedrock upon which you build your culture. These are things you will not sacrifice even if it means the mission will fail.

Values may be words like:

Communication
Respect
Integrity
Excellence

Hard to argue with these words. Most of you would probably feel good working for an organization with values like these. Actually, none of you would feel good working for the organization that did have these as its values. That organization was Enron. Enron's leadership did not act in line with these values. For them, the end justified the means. In the end, it was their undoing and Enron is gone, leaving behind a trail of pain in its wake.

On the other hand, when Procter & Gamble bought Norwich Eaton, they dropped Charlie Carroll in as general manager. A little while after taking on the assignment, he visited the Norwich operation in Mexico. There he was presented with Norwich's leading drug—the number one selling drug in all of Mexico.

"What does it do?"

"It's a placebo. In your country doctors say 'take two aspirin and call me in the morning'. Here doctors have people take two of these and call them in the morning. It works half the time. And because it's a placebo, it has absolutely no side effects. Anyone can take it."

"Pull it off the market immediately."

Charlie didn't hesitate. Charlie didn't have to call anyone at headquarters to clear his decision. He knew that continuing to sell a placebo was in fundamental violation of Procter & Gamble's commitment to doing the right thing.

At one point another Procter & Gamble employee had presented P&G's VP of advertising, Richard Goldstein, with what he thought was a tough choice. Richard didn't see it that way at all.

"Let's do this."

"But that will cost us business."

"Principles are only principles when they hurt."

This is the difference between hollow words on a wall and values in action.

TOOL 5.3
VALUES

What will we not sacrifice on the way to achieving our mission and vision?

Perhaps get there with a shield exercise:

1. Each participant creates his or her own personal shield with the answers to some or all of the following in words, pictures, or a combination.

Favorite

- Person (hero)
- Place (location)
- Possession (thing you own)
- Principles (values)
- Pastime (activity)
- Present (gift)
- Fantasy (dream for the future)
- Source of pride (motivator)

2. Participants share their shields, explaining why they chose what they chose. Because . . .
3. Facilitator listens for and records values behind the choices.
4. Facilitator puts captured values on Post-it notes on wall.
5. Participants group values into core clusters, agreeing on overall label for each cluster.

Copyright © PrimeGenesis® LLC. To customize this document, download Tool 5.3 from the First-Time Leader page on www.onboardingtools.com.

COHERENCE

Mission, vision, and values are different—but yours need to be congruent. If you run an organization that does assassinations for hire, it probably doesn't make sense to have the sanctity of life as a core value. If you run an organization that is in the business of managing nuclear power plants once they are up and running, it probably doesn't make sense to have never doing things the same way twice as a core value.

SUMMARY: WHAT MATTERS

Get the team aligned around a coherent shared purpose

- Mission
- Vision
- Values

Once you define what matters and what the end game is, and the team is on board, decisions become more straightforward, and there is buy-in from the team (sometimes even in hard times).

Chapter 6

ATTITUDE: MAKE CRUCIAL CHOICES AROUND YOUR TEAM'S STRATEGY, POSTURE, AND CULTURE

This chapter gets at the critical choices driving how first-time leaders and their teams will win—strategy, posture, and culture. Like your mission, vision, and values, these need to form a coherent direction.

STRATEGY

At its core, strategy is about generating and selecting options to close gaps between objectives and current realities. It is about the creation and allocation of resources to the right place, in the right way, at the right time, over time that bring to fruition your mission, vision, objectives, and goals while maintaining values.

Your task as the leader is to lead the team in creating and selecting the most effective set of strategic options that will get you from your current reality to your desired destination. In addition to the gap between where you are and where you want to be there will most likely be some barriers keeping that gap in place. Your strategy should guide the actions that your team takes to bridge that gap and eliminate those barriers.

Michael Porter suggests that almost any industry's value chain includes design, produce, sell, deliver, and support. A big part of strategy is identifying and playing to the organization's unique strengths relative to its competitors at one point on the value chain.

Innovation Follow-Through—Richard Branson

Richard Branson has achieved remarkable success taking the Virgin brand into industries "out of frustration" with existing record, airline, and telecommunication companies, and the like. He looks for "obvious gaps in the market" and launches products or services that are "heads above everyone else." To continue to succeed (in industries that don't "get killed by a technological change"), he says, "The way you survive is to be much more creative than your rivals."[1]

When pushed, Branson described the Virgin Cola example:

> Virgin Cola was our greatest success in that we were so successful in the UK that we absolutely terrified Coke. They sent a 747 with bag loads of money and 20 SWAT teams to the UK and we suddenly found it disappearing from all the shelves. They decided just to stop the company completely before we could get going out around the world. Because you've got two cans of soft drink, although people at the time preferred the Virgin brand of cola—we were outselling them and Pepsi at 3:1—we didn't have a fundamentally better product. When British Airways tried to do that to us in the aviation business, we were able to beat them. We were not in soft drinks.

It's one of Branson's main themes. As he said in a recent graduation speech,[2] "We always enter markets where the leaders are not doing a great job, so we can go in and disrupt them by offering better quality services." Now he's so tired of waiting for NASA that he's launching his own space travel program. This is definitely a man who reaches for the stars over and over again.

For Branson, it's about being "much more creative than our rivals" (design). For others it's about producing better or delivering better or providing superior customer service. You and your team need to figure out the strategy for how you are going to win.

The Six-Step Strategic Planning Process

The following six-step process will allow you to create a complete and robust strategic plan. We are not suggesting that this is the only way to do this. But it is a good way.

1. Set an aspirational destination (derived from the mission and vision).
2. Assess the facts of the current reality and develop potential future scenarios.
3. Identify options to bridge gaps between the current reality and the desired aspiration.
4. Evaluate options under different scenarios. Make choices.
5. Develop detailed plans that will deliver on selected strategies.
6. Act, measure, adjust, and repeat.

Set the Aspirational Destination
Strategic planning begins with the aspirational long-term destination, which should be derived directly from the mission and vision. It is important for this step to come before looking at the current reality. Starting with the current reality tends to limit thinking and produce incremental results. Starting with the end in mind encourages bigger ideas.

Assess the Facts of the Current Reality and Develop Future Scenarios
The next step is to analyze the current reality. This involves reviewing, once again, the 5Cs (Customers, Collaborators, Capabilities, Competitors, and Conditions) as well as performing a SWOT (Strengths, Weaknesses, Opportunities, Threats) analysis.

Developing scenarios is an exercise in trying to foresee potential changes in the environment (social, political, demographic, organizational, economic, etc.) that might impact your strategic choices. The changes are generally outside the control of the organization or the team—particularly in today's era of ever-accelerating technological change. Given this, the organization cannot choose which scenario will happen, but it can estimate the probabilities of each scenario happening. This can help determine the expected results of different strategic options.

Identify Options to Bridge Gaps between Reality and Aspiration
Next, determine what strategic options might create additional value (or in some cases, minimize its destruction). Be creative, thinking out of the box so you can come up with a range of options that can potentially address the issues and move the organization forward. For ideas, look at your key leverage points for offensive options and at your key business issues for defensive options.

This is a good time to get stakeholder input. You are trying to generate ideas. So if your stakeholders have good ideas, you want to know about them. Keep in mind that at this stage you are not looking for decisions, just input and options.

Evaluate Options under Different Scenarios
In this step determine which options create the most risk-adjusted value over time, under different scenarios. Evaluate options and scenarios leading to a range of forecasts based on transparent assumptions. At this point, involve key stakeholders to understand and to help improve the components of the valuation assumptions.

For example, assume three scenarios for the future of the industry:

1. Industry consolidation: Number of customers shrinking
2. Industry stagnation: Number of customers constant
3. Industry expansion: Number of customers increasing

To determine which of your options has the highest expected value, figure out what the payoff will be under each scenario and what the probabilities will be of each happening.

Eventually get the key stakeholders involved to agree on which options to pursue.

After a complete evaluation, decide on your core strategic choices that will clearly define where the organization will focus its efforts and how it will win versus its competition. Aim to have three to five strategic choices that will deliver 75 percent of the goals.

Develop Detailed Business Plans

With your strategic choices in place, develop a detailed business plan that addresses the strategic, operational, and organizational actions that are needed to implement each selected option. For each strategic choice, consider resource requirements and allocation, rules of engagement, critical business drivers, timetables, roles, responsibilities, capability enhancements, performance management plans, accountability, standards, measures, and goals.

Act, Measure, Adjust, and Repeat

Once the detailed business plan is in play continually monitor its progress against your stated goals to ensure what you thought would happen is happening in a timely manner.

To ensure that the team members remain on target to get to their aspirational destination,

Get milestones in place immediately. Track them and manage them as a team on a frequent and regular basis. Don't underestimate the power of celebrating early wins.

Adjust as necessary. This whole process is about you and your team together. Your team must feel like they're part of the process but so too must your key stakeholders. Remember to include your stakeholders by

- Obtaining their input to enhance scenarios and options. Engage with them and capture their ideas.
- Involving them to help understand and to improve valuation assumptions. Tap into their experience and context.
- Gaining their agreement on which options to pursue. (This should naturally occur as a result of the expected valuation of different options under different scenarios.)

Strategic Planning Summary

Strategic planning begins with the aspirational destination that is drawn from the vision and mission:

Analyze the current reality by using the 5Cs approach.
Complete a SWOT summary.
Create strategy options to guide actions, overcome barriers, and bridge gaps.
Get key stakeholders' input into options and assumptions.
Get key stakeholders' agreement on which strategic options to pursue.
Develop a business plan with strategic, operational, and organizational actions
    that are needed to implement each selected option.

TOOL 6.1
STRATEGIC PLANNING

Input
    4.1 Situation assessment—5Cs
    4.2 SWOT
    4.3 Profit pools
    4.4 Where to play choices
    5.1 Mission
    5.2 Vision
    5.3 Values

1. Set the aspirational destination (flows from mission and vision).
2. Assess the facts of the current reality (from situation assessment, SWOT, profit pools) and develop future scenarios:
    Scenario 1
    Scenario 2
    Scenario 3
3. Identify options to bridge gaps between reality and aspiration.
    Option 1
    Option 2
    Option 3
    • Peer and management input to enhance scenarios and options
4. Evaluate options under different scenarios.
    • Peer and management involvement to understand and improve valuation assumptions
    • Management agreement on which options to pursue
5. Develop detailed business plans.
6. Act, measure, adjust, and repeat.

The business planning tool (Tool 6.2) is closely related to the strategic planning tool, putting more detail on some of the elements. Use the two tools together.

TOOL 6.2
BUSINESS PLAN ELEMENTS

Strategic Plan
    Strategic posture: shape, adapt, reserve:
    Resource allocation:
    Rules of engagement across critical business drivers:

Resource Plan (requirements, application, sources)
    Human:
    Financial:
    Technical:
    Operational:

Action Plan

	Actions	Timing	Responsibilities	Linkages
Near-term				
Long-term				

Performance Management Plan
    Operating and financial performance standards:

    Measures and goals:

POSTURE

An important part of how to win is your organization's posture. It turns out that not every organization should be the most proactive. Certainly organizations hanging their hat on design like Virgin or Apple must be proactive. But organizations like the Coca-Cola Company are better off as fast followers. Still others like the Red Cross focus on preparing in advance to react when disasters hit. And service-focused organizations like the Ritz pride themselves on their ability to respond to guests' needs.

Strategic Plank	Design	Produce	Deliver	Support
Example Organization	Apple	Coca-Cola	Red Cross	Ritz
Posture	Proactive	Fast follow	Prepared	Responsive

For example, leveraging service as a strategic weapon requires the right attitude and superior discipline. Only organizations with a "service first" mentality can even hope to create a service advantage. But that's not enough. You must combine that with superior discipline in executing against something like ClickSoftware CEO Moshe BenBassat's W6 questions: *Who does what for whom with what, where, and when?*

He explained this to George for one of his Forbes.com columns.[3]

On one level, BenBassat's W6 merely take basic milestone management up a notch beyond *what is getting done by whom when.* However, when it comes to service delivery you do need more than basics. While manufacture planning concerns scheduling machines and materials, service planning requires more sophisticated time management and skill optimization.

BenBassat's first "aha moment" was sparked by his work helping the Israeli air force assemble its annual schedule. The existing process involved *putting four smart officers in a room and not letting them out until they had a solution* to optimize planes, fuel, exercises, and people's time. This took months, literally. Instead, BenBassat built a software solution which leveraged artificial intelligence to do what the officers did—but in minutes.

We'll leave it to BenBassat to explain the software, focusing here on applying BenBassat's W6 logic to your service planning, regardless of the problem you are trying to solve.

For Whom?

Begin with the client of your service. This is another form of the BRAVE leadership question, Where to play? Note that the more demanding customers are not necessarily the highest priority. "First come, first served" and "The squeakiest wheel gets oiled first" are not value-creating strategies.

Gillian will never forget these two statements she kept in the back of her mind from business school:

- 80 percent of your business comes from 20 percent of your customers.
- It's much easier to keep an existing customer than it is to secure a new one.

Her first step when she started was to get a previous and existing client list and started her business development strategy from there.

What?

With the client in mind, get clear on what services you are going to provide—and not provide.

Who?

Service is delivered by people with unequal skills. As BenBassat experienced in his work with utility companies, the skills required to install are different from those required to repair. Find the person with the right skills and temperament to deliver the specific service required.

With What?

Service requires resources. We've all experienced plumbers assessing a problem and then leaving to retrieve the required parts. To properly leverage service, ensure your people have the tools and materials they need when they need them.

Where?

There's been a fundamental shift in where some services are delivered. Sometimes it still makes sense to go where the need is (e.g., doctor house calls). Other times, it's better to have the need brought to you (e.g., hospital operations). Make a considered choice.

When?

Not all service requires immediate delivery and delivering ASAP is expensive. In many instances, the monetary cost advantages in batching service delivery outweigh the customer satisfaction cost of delay.

BenBassat's W6 *Who does what for whom with what, where, and when?* is a valuable framework which can be used to leverage service as a strategic weapon—especially if one combines discipline with the right attitude in terms of strategy, posture, and culture.

And in today's competitive economy, where many companies can no longer rely on product or pricing as a differentiator, it is the service experience that is influencing buying decisions.

Think through which posture is appropriate for the strategy you and your team have chosen.

TOOL 6.3
POSTURE MAPPING

	Proactive	Fast Follow	Prepared	Responsive
Element				

Copyright © PrimeGenesis® LLC. To customize this document, download Tool 6.3 from the First-Time Leader page on www.onboardingtools.com.

CULTURE

U.S. Army colonel Randy Chase spent 10 days on a navy ship for cross training. On his second day, he ran out of toothpaste, so he went over to the ship's store to buy another tube. The stores on navy ships aren't as big as your typical suburban supermarket (only two people can fit in the store at a time), so there was a short line to get in. He went to the end of the line and said good morning to the man in front of him, who took one look at him and ran away. Almost immediately, a navy lieutenant appeared and asked, "Colonel, sir. What are you doing?"

What had he done wrong?

Colonel Chase had done two things wrong. (1) Officers don't talk to enlisted men on ships except to convey orders. (2) Officers don't wait in lines.

True. True. This incident took place in the last century. But the cultural differences between the services are still there. As Boris Groysberg, Andrew Hill, and Toby Johnson describe in "Which of These People Is Your Future CEO?" in the November 2010 *Harvard Business Review*, the navy and air force are strong on process and light on flexibility, while the army and marines are lighter on process and stronger on flexibility. They argue these differences stem from the toys with which the different services play. A small mistake on a ship can have devastating impact, as can not reacting to a changing situation in ground warfare.

There are some deep-seated cultural differences in organizations that have their roots in the context in which those organizations operate. It's important for first-time leaders to understand what drives behaviors, relationships, and attitudes before trying to fight them or change them.

An organization's culture underpins "The way we do things here" and is made up of BRAVE (Behaviors, Relationships, Attitudes, Values, and Environment). Just as an individual has preferences, so, too, does an organization. The BRAVE cultural framework and tool will help you (a) understand the existing organizational preferences, and (b) evolve them in a coherent fashion.

When it comes to culture, use dimensions like these. (This is one of those areas to adapt for your specific situation.)

Environment
- World/market perspective: ignored versus sought out
- Colleagues' perspective: ignored (signaled by walls and formal décor) versus sought out (signaled by open plan and informal décor)
- Historical organizational perspective: ignored versus sought out

Values
- Buy-in to purpose: not much versus fully committed
- Learning: directive versus collaborative/shared
- Risk appetite: protect what is/have versus risk more/gain more
- Underlying beliefs:

Attitude
- Strategy: win with execution versus win with innovation
- Posture: reactive/responsive versus proactive
- Approach: disciplined versus flexible

Relationships
- Power/decision making: controlled/monarchical versus diffused with open debate and conflict
- Communication/controls: formal, directed, written versus informal, verbal, face-to-face
- Identity: subgroup bias versus one-team bias

Behaviors
- Unit: individual versus team based
- Discipline: structured/disciplined versus fluid/flexible
- Focus: internally focused versus externally integrated

Not surprisingly, when you apply these criteria to the army you get a very different picture than you do with the navy. It's not that one is better than the other. It's just that they are different—as should be the culture in the operating room and disease diagnosing rooms of the same hospital.

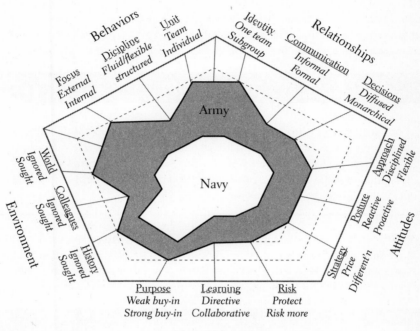

People generally learn about culture starting with the most superficial (what people say about their culture), but it is rooted in what people really are, their core assumptions and beliefs—Be. Do. Say. This approach can be applied to people individually and to organizations on a whole. Let's take a deeper look at each element.

Be: The underpinning of culture (and integrity) is what people really are, their core assumptions, beliefs, and intentions. These show up in *attitudes* and *values.*

Do: These are behavioral, attitudinal, and communication norms that can be seen, felt, or heard such as signs and symbols like physical layouts, the way people dress, talk to each other, and interact with each other. These show up in *behaviors, relationships,* and the work *environment.*

Say: What people say about their culture can be found in things like mission statements, creeds, and stories. As Edgar Schein points out, these get at the professed culture.[4]

For a culture to be sustainable, the BRAVE elements and what people say, do, and are must be in sync. It is easy to see when people's behaviors don't match their words. It is far more difficult to figure out when their words and behaviors match each other, but don't match underlying values. Yet, when that happens, those people's behaviors, relationships, and attitudes will change over time. Just as your own values, actions, and words need to line up, the same is true for those of an organization.

BRAVE TIP

Look well beyond the professed culture: it's not what people like about their preferences. It's just that value statements and creeds are often aspirational. You must understand the resting, steady-state norms of behaviors, relationships, attitudes, values, and the work environment that people default to when the boss is not around.

According to True Value CEO Lyle Heidemann, changing a corporate culture is a five-year effort.[5] He also said that it doesn't seem to work well to attack behaviors or relationships head on. It's very hard to evolve values quickly, and generally speaking it is expensive to change the environment. That leaves attitude.

Implications for you:
1. Start with the cause, the why. Get all aligned around your *purpose*. Make sure all believe in its import and are committed to a common vision.
2. Reconfirm where to play choices, within the ever-changing *environmental* context.
3. Reconfirm the organization's core *values*, trying to change them only if absolutely necessary.
4. Then adjust your *attitude*, relooking at strategic priorities, posture, and culture and how they sync.
5. Once everyone understands the attitudinal choices, relook at *relationships* and *behaviors* through that lens, evolving them as dictated by the new attitude.

TOOL 6.4
CULTURE ASSESSMENT

Environment—Where to Play

World/Market Perspective

Ignored ......|......|......|......|......|...... Sought out

Colleagues Perspective

Ignored/walls/formal ......|......|......|......|......|...... Sought out/open/informal

Historical Organizational Perspective

Ignored ......|......|......|......|......|...... Sought out
Other insights:

Values—What Matters

Buy-In to Purpose

Not much ......|......|......|......|......|..... Fully Committed

Learning

Directive ....|......|......|......|......|...... Collaborative/shared

Risk Appetite

Protect what is ......|......|......|......|......|...... Risk more/gain more
Underlying beliefs:

Attitude—How to Win

Strategy

Win with execution ......|......|......|......|......|...... Win with innovation

Posture

Reactive/responsive ......|......|......|......|......|...... Proactive

(continued)

Approach

Disciplined ......|......|......|......|......|...... Flexible
Other observations:

Relationships—How to Connect

Power Decision Making

Controlled/monarchical ......|......|......|......|......|...... Diffused/open debate
and conflict

Communication/Controls

Formal/directed/written ......|......|......|......|......|...... Informal/verbal/
face-to-face

Identity

Subgroup bias ......|......|......|......|......|...... One-team bias
Others:

Behaviors—What Impact

Unit

Individual ......|......|......|......|......|...... Team-based

Discipline

Structured/disciplined ......|......|......|......|......|...... Fluid/flexible

Focus

Internally focused ......|......|......|......|......|...... Externally integrated
Others:

Copyright © PrimeGenesis® LLC. To customize this document, download Tool
6.4 from the First-Time Leader page on www.onboardingtools.com.

SUMMARY: HOW TO WIN

- Clarify strategy, generating and selecting options that will close the gaps between the objectives and current reality.
- Think through which posture is appropriate for the strategy you and your team have chosen.
- Choose your BRAVE culture across behaviors, relationships, attitudes, values, and environment.
- Make sure your strategy, posture, and culture reinforce each other.

Chapter 7

RELATIONSHIPS: THE HEART OF LEADERSHIP

The most important moments of impact involve one human being connecting with another human being. The relationship could be emotionally charged, direct, or indirect. Either way, what you've thought through and done before sets up the moment of impact and what happens afterwards.

Setting up, managing, and following through from those moments of impact well requires a tremendous amount of thinking and work. Thus this is our longest chapter. It could be overwhelming. So we've broken it into sections:

Communication Frameworks (Tools 7.1 to 7.4),
How to Hire Great People (Tools 7.5 to 7.13),
Bringing New Hires into the Team (Tools 7.14 to 7.17), and
Managing People Who Are Doing Well—and Not So Well (Tools 7.18 to 7.25).

The last three all fit inside ADEPT people management (Acquire, Develop, Encourage, Plan, Transition).

In many ways, this is the heart of inspiring and enabling others.

COMMUNICATION FRAMEWORKS

Let's begin by putting in place some frameworks.

Engagement: Compliant–Contributing–Committed

Crossing the secret of happiness (good for others, good for me, good at it, as outlined in Chapter 5) and Maslow's hierarchy of needs produces a way to look at different levels of engagement—disengaged, compliant, contributing, committed.

Disengaged—Those disengaged or engaged with the wrong things hurt the organization. They don't meet the minimum standards and distract others.

Compliant—At the first level of engagement, compliant people do no harm. They show up. They observe. They focus on what's good for me and meet the minimum requirements to satisfy their biological and physiological needs.

Contributing—One level up, contributors do things they are good at. They collaborate with others and help as they seek belonging and self-esteem.

Committed—At the highest level are the people trying to do good for others. They care about the organization's purpose and teach others as part of their own self-actualization.

Communication Levels: Emotional–Direct–Indirect

Moving people through from disengaged to compliant to contributing to committed requires different levels of communication.

Indirect communication can build awareness and enough understanding for people to be able to comply with requests and direction.

Direct communication can build the understanding that enables people to make active contributions.

Emotional communication can change what people believe and how they feel as part of inspiring their commitment to an idea or cause.

Persuasion

Bryan Smith lays out different ways of persuading people in a section in *The Fifth Discipline Fieldbook*[1]): tell–sell–test–consult–co-create. We have found that

Telling someone to do something yields compliance at best.
Selling, testing, and consulting sets people up to contribute.
Co-creating is one of the best ways to engender commitment.

Self-Awareness

Communication begins with self-awareness. Some thoughts on this:

- You can't lead until you know yourself.
- Know how your communication style affects others.
- Recognize different styles in others, and pull out their strengths.

With high self-awareness comes high self-confidence. Self-aware beings are assured of their decisions; they are aware of their strengths as well as their weaknesses, and are not embarrassed by that.

When confidence shines through, others will follow. When Gillian first started as a leader, she was scared, mostly of the unknown, but a lot of it had to do with thinking, "I'm not sure if I'm doing the right thing." One of her team members came up to her after a meeting and told her, "What are you afraid of? I can tell you're uncomfortable. We are part of your team and we support you. You are in this position because you can do this." It was what she needed to hear, and she was fortunate to start off in a team that not only supported her but also believed in her. Over the next few weeks, she worked hard at building confidence, doing a series of exercises, seeing coaches, and so on. Her leadership abilities skyrocketed once she started believing in herself. It all started to come naturally.

Confidence is not to be mistaken for arrogance. As a leader, leave your ego at the door. The success of your team will determine the size of your ego.

Starting with herself, Gillian moved through her team, getting to know them, recognizing their personal styles. Everyone is different and reacts to different triggers. A blanket approach won't work. Introverts respond differently than extroverts, and don't ever expect either type to work otherwise. By taking the time to get to know each style on her team, Gillian was able to pull people into different projects that played to their strengths. Morale was boosted. Co-creation was abundant. Projects were completed with new insights. Goals were met. It's win-win.

Communication is the foundation of successful relationships, both in business and in our personal lives. Excel at communicating with different styles.

Communication is not a one-time event. To change how people feel, think in terms of a communication MAP—Message, Amplifiers, Perseverance.

Message
Frame your message by thinking through the platform for change, vision, and call to action. Then distill those components down to one driving message and three communication points.

No one will do anything differently until they (a) believe they must change, (b) can picture themselves in a brighter future, and (c) see how they can be part of the solution.

> **Platform for change:** The things that will make your audience realize they need to do something different from what they have been doing.
> **Vision:** Picture of a brighter future—in which your audience can picture themselves.
> **Call to action:** Actions the audience can take to get there.

To illustrate these points, imagine a pack of polar bears. They are playing on an ice flow. It's melting! It's drifting out to sea! The bears either are going to drown or starve to death. Neither scenario is good (platform for change). However there is some food nearby sitting on land. The bears could play there, be safe, and get food (vision). So, the lead polar bears come up with a plan to depart the drifting ice and safely swim to land (call to action).

Keep in mind that everyone who is affected by your leadership will want to know the same thing: How will the changes impact me? So, when you are crafting your communication points, be sure to be able to explain (1) how the changes will affect them and (2) how the changes enable them to be more successful themselves.

Great communication pivots off a central message.

For example, "We're going to be 1 or 2 or we're going to get out" was one of Jack Welch's early messages at GE.

Or, "A car in every driveway" was the overarching message Ford deployed early in the twentieth century.

The purpose of an overarching message is to anchor everything else in your communication plan. A good place to find it is in your vision of the future.

Writing about Jean Claude Brizard—Rochester, New York's, new school superintendent at the time—Meaghan McDermott said,

> His message for Rochester is that we must "make education personal."
>
> "I read somewhere once that every child is a work of art," he said.
>
> "Our task is to help create a masterpiece out of each. We need to get teachers and principals to a place where they can track the progress of each student and create the proper enrichment and intervention for each."
>
> He said he wants to create an environment in the district where if he asks a school principal about a specific student and their dreams, aspirations, struggles, and achievement, he and school leaders will be able to have a meaningful dialogue about that child's future.[2]

Amplifiers

Amplifiers include the people that will help you drive your message and the media you leverage. There are always others influencing the people you want to influence. Think through stakeholders all around the people you want to influence including their bosses, peers, subordinates, mentors, advisers, and the like. Find and deploy like-thinking allies in your quest.

The media you select are the methods or vehicles you choose to deliver your message. It is more common to distribute your message through multiple media. The options have exploded in quantity and kind, each one with slightly different effects on how the message is perceived. What people often fail to consider is that the same medium will have different effects on different people with different messages.

There is great opportunity here, and great danger. The same message sent via a press release will be perceived differently than the exact same message sent via Twitter or Facebook. A creative or fun free-for-all with a listserv can be great for some communication efforts—a friendly rivalry—and disastrous for others, like communicating a change in organizational structure. It's worth slowing down and thinking through the message, the media, and your goals carefully.

Media will fall into one of three main types: two-way, alternating, and one-way.

Two-Way Media   When it really matters, when the personal stakes are high; when you need to deploy words, tone, and body language to their fullest potential; and when you really need to soak in the other's words, tone, and body language you need two-way media. First prize is face-to-face, one-on-one, in the same space.

The ease and seeming intimacy of certain new media—e-mail, texts—can lead to a fateful error of judgment about not using face-to-face, one-on-one communication when it should be used. A recent campaign for smartphones spoofs on such errors when a woman breaks up with her romantic partner by texting him while he sits across the table from her. Almost no one ever regrets lifting his or her fingers off the keyboard, getting out of his or her office, and walking over, driving over, or flying over to have a face-to-face, one-on-one conversation. Choosing this correctly is a matter of leadership.

Small-group meetings are particularly useful for pulling together diverse groups to solve problems, explore issues, and have multiplayer conversations. Medium- and large-group meetings and events are useful for disseminating knowledge and answering some questions live.

Videoconferences and video chat can communicate words, tone, and some body language without traveling. And phone is good for two-way communication of words and tone (but no body language).

Alternating Media   These are one-way media that allow for almost instantaneous response. Indeed, they are so fast that they often feel like simultaneous two-way media. These include things like online chat, text messages, and all sorts of new media being invented as you read. Use them. But don't mistake them for true two-way media.

One-Way Media   Mass and social media are useful for disseminating information broadly, quickly. The list is endless and includes things like Facebook, LinkedIn, blogs, Twitter, network sites, news feeds, bulletin boards, posters, television, radio, print, video, voicemail, e-mail, hand-written notes, and, not to forget, books.

Perseverance

Manage your communication plan as an iterative set of concurrent conversations around a set of topics that you propose and guide. Shape it as best you can, but know that in most cases some element of your communication network will always be taking on a direction of its own, including ones you didn't anticipate or possibly may not like.

Be acutely aware of how different media get different results. If you really aren't interested in people airing their opinions about the newly announced merger, don't invite it. If you feel that you have a culture that can embrace this and can convert it to a positive energy-building activity, then you might want to consider it.

For all these reasons, you're going to need to stick with your communication, driving your message over and over again at different times, with different people, in different ways.

The Red Cross's Charley Shimanski[3]

Charley Shimanski's words inspire. His actions inspire. And they hold together because he firmly believes the importance of what he says and does. He exemplifies how new leaders can—and should—develop and implement communication efforts that inspire others to embrace and execute their missions. To put it simply, Be. Do. Say.

George had the opportunity to spend some time with Charley at his first Red Cross Disaster Response Directors Conference. He had recently moved from being CEO of the Red Cross's Denver chapter to heading up the organization's overall disaster response. This was his onboarding coming out party with his top 180 or so leaders. He knew that what he communicated and how he communicated it would be critical. But he wasn't worried about it.

The reason he wasn't worried was that the Red Cross's mission is core to his being. George asked Charley what was most important to him. He didn't hesitate:

> Our people. They are not only the most important asset we have, they are what makes the American Red Cross what it is. They represent that segment of society that is willing to roll up its sleeves to help someone that that they've never met before.

Charley went on to describe his thought process in preparing for the conference:

> I start by getting a sense of what I want them to feel when they're done hearing from me—what I want them to feel, not hear me say. . . . I wanted them to feel that they are at the core of what we do, that our success is on their shoulders. I wanted them to feel proud.

He reinforced his sense of pride in the Red Cross on a continual basis throughout the conference, talking about how the organization is often "the best part of someone's worst day," and punctuating others' success stories with "How cool is that? You should feel that that's pretty cool. I hope you do."

He also shared his own stories, describing how he first volunteered for disaster response 25 years ago when he saw a local TV news broadcast about a boy lost in the Colorado mountains and just showed up and helped.

Charley went on to discuss how he spent 25 years as a member of Colorado's Alpine Rescue Team and a stint as president of the national Mountain Rescue Association; he mentioned how much the Red Cross has meant to him at very specific times in his life, particularly as a recipient of help from the Red Cross when he volunteered as a first-responder on rescues:

> There's no better cup of coffee than the cup of coffee served in a cardboard cup with a Red Cross on it because it's a cup of love.

Charley physically and emotionally puts his arms around people and draws them close to him, making them feel better about themselves. He does this face-to-face, one-on-one, and with his equally inspiring boss, Red Cross president and CEO Gail McGovern. Both of them reinforce the notion that disaster response is at "the heart of the Red Cross's mission." He reinforces this message continually in large groups, interviews, and through his Twitter account—warning people of risks, cajoling them to help, and complimenting good work.

Charley tells the story of people in a restaurant who hear the sound of a significant car accident. As he describes it,

- Many will go to the window to see what happened.
- Some will go to the curb to see what happens next.
- But a small number of those patrons will rush to the accident scene to *be* what happens next—helping out however they can to the best of their abilities.

Charley and the people he inspires through his communications are those who want to *be* what happens next. Be. Do. Say.

Everything Communicates

Not surprisingly, since we live in the midst of a communication revolution, the guidelines for communicating are changing dramatically. As much as we would like to treat communication as a logical, sequential, ongoing communication campaign, in many cases, it's more essential to manage it as an iterative set of concurrent conversations:

- Take into account the network of multiple stakeholders as you specifically identify your target audiences.
- Discover and leverage your overarching message as the foundation for guiding iterative concurrent conversations by seeding and reinforcing

communication points through a wide variety of media with no compromises on trustworthiness and authenticity.

- Monitor and adjust as appropriate on an ongoing basis.

Don't hesitate to deploy an old school logical, sequential communication campaign when appropriate—though we expect that to be the case less and less over time.

Charley inspires—as should you.

Business Presenting 101

Sandy Linver built a whole expertise on presenting and communicating and shared it with people all around the world through her Speakeasy organization. This section relies heavily on that. Most of the ideas are hers, with some adaptation.[4]

Her basic framework is that presenting is about bridging gaps. Start by figuring out what the impact on your audience needs to be. Then figure out where they are now. Then move them to where they need to be. The steps are

1. Identify your destination.

   Think through what impact you want to make on your audience. How do you want them to react? How do you want them to feel? What do you want them to do? Get specific about what you want them to understand, believe, say, and do.

2. Be explicit about unstated Xs.

   There's also a hidden X. Your audience won't buy what you're selling until they buy you. So, think through how you want your audience to think and feel about you.

3. Assess current reality.

   Next, get real about your starting point. Figure out where your audience is now. What are they aware of; what do they understand, believe? Which aspects of that help your cause? Which get in the way? You need to understand where they are and how and why they got there.

   At the same time, develop a risk management plan. Assume things are not going to go exactly as you'd hoped. (They rarely do.) Think through potential obstacles, negative rumors, hecklers or other sabotage, legal requirements, and unintended consequences of what you say or do. Scenario planning is often helpful.

4. Reevaluate destination in light of assumptions about audience.

   Now go back and relook at your destination. Given what you just laid out about the current reality, can you still get all the way to the target you set in section 1? Or do you need to get there in steps?

5. Bridge the gap.

   This is the core of the communication strategy—choosing what you need to communicate to bridge the gap between the current reality and your destination. Think through what people need to be aware of, understand, believe, and feel to move from current reality to your destination.

6. Develop core ideas and key communication points (maximum five core ideas).

This flows right out of your section 5 strategy to bridge the gap. It's not about what you want to say. It's about how they need to feel to move in the direction you want them to go.

7. Package the message.

Now you're ready to start packaging your message, thinking through
   - How should core ideas be packaged for optimum effectiveness?
   - What kind of supporting data do you need?
   - What is your key opening idea?
   - What is your key closing idea?

8. Deliver the message.

And, with that, you're ready to think through and implement your delivery. Think through what are the best vehicles to reach your audience or constituents. Think through what is the optimum combination of those vehicles. Make choices about the best timing to release the message. Get clear on who and what influences whom. This is where you pull in your amplifiers. And don't forget to plan out how you can best plant the follow-up seeds.

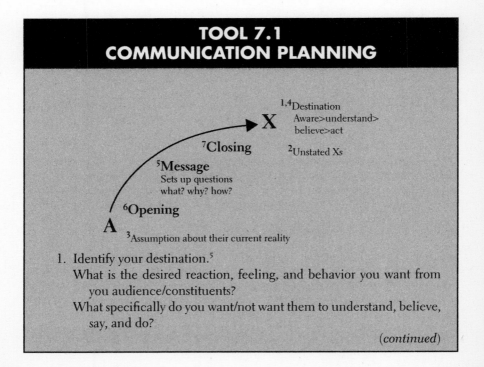

TOOL 7.1
COMMUNICATION PLANNING

X [1,4]Destination
Aware>understand>
believe>act

[7]Closing   [2]Unstated Xs

[5]Message
Sets up questions
what? why? how?

[6]Opening

A
[3]Assumption about their current reality

1. Identify your destination.[5]

What is the desired reaction, feeling, and behavior you want from you audience/constituents?

What specifically do you want/not want them to understand, believe, say, and do?

(continued)

2. Be explicit about unstated Xs.
   What do you want listener to think and feel about you?
3. Assess current reality.
   What does your audience/constituency currently understand, believe, say? Why?
   Develop a risk management plan including potential obstacles, negative rumors, sabotage, legal requirements, unintended consequences, and scenarios.
4. Reevaluate destination in light of assumptions about audience.
5. Bridge the gap.
   What do people need to be aware of, understand, believe, and feel to move from current reality to your destination?
6. Develop core ideas and key communication points (maximum five core ideas).
7. Package the message.
   How should core ideas be packaged for optimum effectiveness?
   What kind of supporting data do you need?
   What is your key opening idea?
   What is your key closing idea?
8. Deliver the message.
   What are the best vehicles to reach your audience or constituents?
   What is the optimum combination?
   What is the best timing to release the message?
   Who and what influences whom—amplifiers?
   How do you best plant the follow-up seeds?

Copyright © PrimeGenesis® LLC. To customize this document, download Tool 7.1 from the First-Time Leader page on www.onboardingtools.com.

How Leaders' Communication Styles Impact the Delivery of Results[6]

George asked acoustics expert David Greenberg what the greatest concert hall is. He quickly replied, "For what?" He went on to explain that different venues are better for certain types of performances.

When you think about the best way to communicate with your team, ask yourself, "To do what?" Concert halls designed to accommodate every type of performance become mediocre for each. Similarly, leaders must abandon homogeneous communication strategies. In order to communicate effectively with team members, unite them around your vision; analyze the purpose, constraints, and potential solutions related to your team.

Purpose

Greenberg is president of Westport, Connecticut–based acoustics consultancy Creative Acoustics. He explained to George that different venues are better for small group recitals than for large orchestras or opera or theater or other performance types. Sparing you the technical details, it has to do with both direct and reflected sounds, balance, and reverberation.

According to Greenberg,

> At a certain point it became clear that multi-purpose spaces would need to go from no-purpose (where a single acoustic setting meant a compromise to every use) to truly multi-purpose where significant and ideally simple and quick changes could be made to form a room setting favoring theater to one required by symphony, or opera or film or dance or . . .

A leader's communication strategy varies depending upon a team's purpose, strategy, and posture. Communication with teams possessing dominant market positions will likely be more formal, systematic, and direct, in line with the discipline required to maintain that top position. Conversely, teams playing niches or creating completely new things will be better served by a more informal, adaptive, and reflective approach.

Constraints

The constraints inherent in making truly multipurpose venues are substantial. One must consider regulations and code requirements, in addition to basic needs like lighting angles, temperature, sightlines, aesthetics, and budget.

One major constraint for leaders will be the organization and community environment in which teams operate. Team communication nests within accepted norms. But those create an all-purpose/no-purpose hall that, almost by definition, is a compromise.

Solutions

The answer to creating an effective multipurpose venue is found in flexible components like orchestra shells and adjustable sound-absorbing materiel deployed when needed and stored when not, creating different sound boxes as appropriate. David makes the point that the sound has to be right for both the audience and the performers.

> Helping the musicians hear themselves and each other is the most important thing because if they are happy they are going to produce the best results.

This is true for high-performing teams as well. As a leader, you need to make sure the people on your team can hear themselves and each other if you want them to produce the best results.

Think in terms of a multipurpose hall, giving different teams and different subteams the ability to modify the box to fit their needs so they can hear themselves and each other better.

Business Writing 101

Consumer products giant Procter & Gamble was famous for its one-page memos. Everyone used the same basic format and same outline for every memo. This meant that readers knew exactly where to find what they were looking for in any memo. Tool 7.2 is an abbreviated guideline to P&G's format of Think–Outline–Write–Edit–Leave–Send (TOWELS)—not a bad starting point for developing your own writing guidelines.

Think   Yes, we are suggesting that you think before you write, just as you should think before you present. Think through the point you want to make. This has two components. The first component is the benefit to the reader. The assumption is that you are writing to communicate something. What? Why will your reader care? What's in it for him or her? Get that clear in your mind before you go any further.

At the same time, think about the image you want to portray of yourself, much like you think through the hidden X in business presenting.

For example, we're choosing to be assertive in this book. While we might soften our tone if we were meeting face-to-face, because we don't have the benefit of tone or body language, we're choosing a harder, more imperative approach to make you stop and think (and implement our ideas). The image we're trying to portray is that of experts sharing knowledge and experience so others can benefit from them.

Different approaches are more appropriate for different situations. (You won't be surprised to learn that the assertive, harder tone of this book generally is less effective with spouses.) So, think through the appropriate approach for your audience and how you want them to perceive you. It's important because your writing needs to communicate your ideas and your personality. They are linked.

Next assemble your evidence. Generally,

- First prize is an analogy. "We did exactly the same thing in exactly the same situation yesterday. Since nothing has changed, it should work today." Or, "This worked in a similar situation . . ."
- Second prize is statistics. "The data suggest . . ."
- Third prize is another credible authority. "George and Gillian say this will work and we should believe them." (In this particular case, if people doubt us, have them give one of us a call. We'll set them straight.)
- Fourth prize is your judgment. This works better the more credibility you have.

Outline   Just as no builder worth his or her salt would start to build a house without a blueprint, shame on you if you start to write without an outline. We spent a month on the 20-page outline for this book, going through innumerable iterations and rethinking and repositioning everything. Your outlines don't need to be that complex. But you need to have them.

The classic P&G memo had six main sections: overview, background, recommendations or conclusions, rationale or findings, discussion, and next steps or indicated actions.

The *overview* is like the first paragraph of a newspaper story, laying out what the note is about, why it's worth reading, when things are going to happen, the benefits and costs, and who else agrees. Note this piece does not include any discussion about how things are going to work. That comes later.

Then step back and fill in the *background*. People who know the background will skip over this piece. Others will be looking for key facts. These should be presented objectively so that anyone looking at these facts should see the same things. As one politician put it, "You are entitled to your own opinions. You are not entitled to your own facts."

Next comes the *recommendation* or *conclusion*. This part trips up a lot of people early on in their business writing endeavors. They think they need to tell the story and lead up to the recommendation. Wrong. Get over it. Readers of business writing want the answer first. Then they're interested in how you got there. If you want to tell stories, write novels or plays. If you want to be a leader, write like a leader.

The recommendation lays out what you're recommending and how it will happen. If you're summarizing research or information, the conclusion lays out what you think—the So what? In neither case should you lay out why this is right. That comes next.

Welcome to next—the *rationale* or *findings*. For a recommendation, this is where you lay out the evidence you collected before. For a summary, this is where you lay out the findings—the "what" you found.

Follow this with a *discussion* of how you're going to make this happen. As appropriate, this is a good place to discuss other alternatives considered but rejected, risks, and contingency plans.

Finally, lay out *next steps* for a recommendation or *indicated actions* for a summary. The difference is that next steps look like "With agreement we will . . ." whereas indicated actions look like "We should . . ."

Write   Write the first draft of your note. We find it more productive to write the whole thing fast as a first draft and go back and revise. Others try to do fewer iterations. We're not sure there's a single best choice here. Write however works for you.

Edit   Do two passes on editing. First do a macro edit to make sure the logic flows and the evidence supports your recommendation or conclusions. Then do a copyedit to get rid of the typppos, grammatical errors, and other minor transgressions.

Leave　This is a big idea. When you think your note is done, walk away. Go do something else. Clear your head. Then, later, come back and read it again. It's amazing how many things look so brilliant late in the evening and so stupid in the first light of the morning. As Joseph Campbell put it, "Regrets are illuminations come too late."[7] Why not let that illumination come sooner rather than later and keep your regrets private?

Send　Now it's done. Send it off.

TOOL 7.2
WRITING GUIDELINES

TOWELS (Think–Outline–Write–Edit–Leave–Send)

Think
　　Think through the point you want to make, benefit to the reader, and image you want to portray of yourself. Assemble your evidence: analogy, statistics, authority, judgment.

Outline
　　Overview: What, why, when, benefits/costs, agreements (not how)
　　Background: Key facts, objectively
　　Recommendation/conclusions: What, how (not why)
　　Rationale/findings: Support for recommendations/conclusions
　　　　(because)—analogy, statistics, authority, judgment
　　Discussion: Expand on how; discuss other alternatives and risks
　　Next steps/indicated actions

Write
Edit
　　Macro edit for evidence and logic
　　Micro edit

Leave
　　Then reread

Send

Meeting Management

It is almost unbelievable how much time people spend in meetings and how much time they waste in bad meetings. We're going to fix that with BRAVE meeting management. Apply the basic prelude, moment of impact, and follow-through approach.

Prelude

Set the overall single objective for the meeting. Note this is not multiple objectives. This is the one overarching objective for the meeting as a whole: inform, discuss, debate, contribute, decide, whatever.

Along with the single overall objective, set clear expectations for learning, contributions, and decisions by agenda item and attendee in line with that single objective. Note this requires an agenda — in advance.

And make sure to get appropriate prework and prereading to people far enough in advance for all to learn/contribute to their fullest potential. This goes to the difference between introverts and extraverts. Extraverts think with their mouths, debating and playing with ideas in real time. Introverts like to mull things over on their own before they open their mouths. If you give everyone materials to read in advance, the extraverts won't read it and will be no worse off in the meeting. The introverts will read it and mull it over and be ready to contribute more in the meeting—which is why you want them there.

Delivery/Moment of Impact

Manage meeting participation and timing to optimize learning, contributions, and action-oriented decisions. This probably means dealing with the most important issues first instead of clicking off the easy ones. It should be clear to everyone walking out of any meeting what their actions are and how they play a part in reaching the overall goal.

Follow-Through

Get meeting notes out promptly to memorialize decisions and actions, kicking off the preparation for the next meeting.

Turning Wasteful Meetings into Drivers of Success[8]

At their best, most meetings are a waste of time. Instead of inspiring and enabling, way too many of them actually drain participants' willingness and ability to do real work. Yet QlikTech has found a way to turn its annual corporate summit into a positive, culture-building and culture-reinforcing event that everyone looks forward to.

When George spoke with QlikTech CEO Lars Bjork for a previous column, Bjork told George that he is "absolutely convinced that [their annual summit] is one critical element to their having been able to sustain a 50 percent Compound Annual Growth Rate for five years."

TOOL 7.3
BRAVE MEETING MANAGEMENT

Behaviors—What impact coming out of the meeting
Relationships—How to connect with people in the meeting
Attitude—How to win in meeting (approach/posture)
Values—What matters (purpose and principles)
Environment—Where to play (context)

Prelude

Set overall single objective:

Set clear expectations for learning, contributions, and decisions by agenda item and attendee in line with that single objective.

Make sure to get appropriate prework and prereading to people far enough in advance for all to learn/contribute to their fullest potential.

Delivery/Moment of Impact

Manage meeting participation and timing to optimize learning, contributions, and action-oriented decisions.

Follow-Through

Get meeting notes out promptly to memorialize decisions and actions, kicking off the preparation for the next meeting.

Brand Experience With that claim in mind, George eagerly accepted QlikTech's invitation to attend one of their annual summits as their guest. From the first drumbeat and emotion of the opening session stories, it was clear that this was no ordinary meeting. QlikTech's head of brand management, Pelle Rosell, had put together each of the 13 summits that QlikTech had had up until then, from the first ski trip with 40 employees to that year's gathering of 1,100 employees in Cancun, Mexico.

Pelle says the event itself is not important. What matters is the "brand experience." Each gathering is the "starting point of every year's journey." For Pelle, enduring branding requires an intersection of organizational values and brand values. He says branding is about belonging. Customers and employees don't so much buy a brand or work for a company as they join it.

Culture as a Journey   For QlikTech, the summit is one critical element in that journey, but just one element. George asked QlikTech's chief people officer Paul Farmer about the other elements:

> *First and foremost, you have to believe what you're saying.* This company believes from top to bottom that *being values-based will deliver performance of people and business.*
>
> When a company starts, its culture is its founder. As it grows, people watch the founder or CEO and follow his or her behaviors, relationships, attitudes, values and environment. At some point, growth means more people, functions, geographies, and complexity across all sorts of dimensions. Along the way, the transmission of culture becomes less personal and more systemic. As Bjork put it, *I used to be able to greet everyone by their first name in the morning. I can't do that anymore.*

Hence the need arose for a chief people officer and a related team to focus on maintaining, evolving, and strengthening QlikTech's winning behaviors not by controlling all the details, but by putting up "guard rails." In particular, Farmer says it's important to embed the company's cultural preferences in core processes like recruiting (values based), onboarding (leveraging the Qlik Academy), performance management, development (including the annual summit), succession planning, and decision making. The more they can do this in a natural way, the more things will stick. This is important because culture is the only truly sustainable competitive advantage.

Rosell likens it to Swiss cheese. As he describes it, culture starts at the top and becomes real in the behaviors of the people on the front line. Middle management is there to transmit ideas and help (inspire and enable). Middle management needs to be a conduit for communication, just like the holes in Swiss cheese are conduits for air. You need to make sure the holes are big enough to allow the important information to pass through, which brings us back to meetings as one of the main conduits of information flows.

IMPLICATIONS FOR YOU

Leverage Five Steps to Effective Meetings

1. **Context.** Understand the meeting's place in the broader journey. It's not about the meeting itself or even the meeting experience. It's about how the meeting moves its participants forward along the path and fits with everything else.
2. **Objective.** Set an overall single objective for the meeting and clear expectations for learning, contributions, and decisions by agenda item and attendee in order to align with the single objective and with the meeting's place in the broader journey.
3. **Prework.** Make sure to get appropriate prework and prereading to people far enough in advance for all to learn/contribute to their fullest potential.
4. **Delivery.** Manage meeting participation and timing to optimize learning, contributions, and action-oriented decisions.
5. **Follow-Through.** Get meeting notes out promptly to memorialize decisions and actions, kicking off the preparation for the next meeting and implementation of decisions and actions.

Press Interviews

If you concentrate on answering the interviewer's questions in a press interview, you're putting your result in their hands. If you're lucky, their agenda matches yours, leading to a happy result.

Don't do that.

Hoping for luck is not a plan.

Instead, concentrate on what you want to communicate and use the interviewer's questions as cues to help you do that. Now you're in charge. And you make the interviewer's job easier. Instead of piecing together a story, he or she can tell your story—with his or her perspective on it.

Net, take control of the interview. Time is on your side if you stay focused on what you want to communicate and you control the dialogue, just as it's on others' sides if they control the dialogue.

George has done a lot of interviews through the years. He continues to be interviewed by others and to interview leaders for his articles for *Forbes* and other publications. He will not go into an interview until he is clear on the slant of the article if he's doing the interview or the three points he wants to make if he's being interviewed. And he's generally transparent about his going-in point of view on the story. He's found it to be helpful because very few people look at interviews as win-lose propositions. Instead, they want to collaborate to craft a valuable story.

In many ways, interviews are moments of impact. Like all moments of impact, think through the prelude, manage the moment, and follow up.

Prepare

Objective—Be clear on the single objective for the interview. What do you want the outcome to be?

Anticipate questions—Know the interviewer, the audience, and their interest factors (competition, conflict, controversy, consequences, familiar person, heartstrings, humor, problem, progress, success, unknown, unusual, wants/needs).

Twitter is a fantastic tool for this. Almost by definition, journalists want people to read what they write. So, many of them Tweet. It's astounding what you can learn about interviewers by reading their recent Tweets. In one case, George figured out that someone who was about to interview him was a rabid Philadelphia sports fan. So George chose Philadelphia sports examples to illustrate the points he made.

Approach—There are always different ways to get to your objective. Figure out the most appropriate approach for the interviewer and his or her audience. This will lead to *key communication points*: get clear on the key points you want to drive (three maximum). This is the most important thing to do to allow you to do more than just answer questions (questions are merely cues for your key points). These points need *support*: facts, personal experience, contrast/compare, analogy, expert opinion, analysis, definition, statistics, and examples (similar to support for writing).

Deliver

Be clear, concise, complete (do one thing well), constructive, credible, controversial, captivating, correct (must correct significant errors on the part of interviewer or press).

Be yourself, liked, prepared, enthusiastic, specific, correct, anecdotal, a listener, a bridge, cool.

Follow Through

Deliver on commitments you make to the interviewer. If you say you're going to send him or her more information, send it. Soon.

Think through what worked particularly well and less well to improve for the future.

TOOL 7.4
PRESS INTERVIEW MANAGEMENT

Prepare

Objective—What do you want out of the interaction?

Anticipate questions—Know interviewer, audience, and their interest factors (competition, conflict, controversy, consequences, familiar person, heartstrings, humor, problem, progress, success, unknown, unusual, wants/needs).

Approach—What way do you choose to go about achieving the objective? There are always different ways to get there. Consider them and choose one. This will lead to *key communication points*: key points you want to drive (three maximum). This will allow you to do more than just answer questions (questions are merely cues for your key points). These points need *support*: facts, personal experience, contrast/compare, analogy, expert opinion, analysis, definition, statistics, and examples.

Deliver

Be clear, concise, complete (do one thing well), constructive, credible, controversial, captivating, correct (must correct significant errors on the part of interviewer or press).

Be yourself, liked, prepared, enthusiastic, specific, correct, anecdotal, a listener, a bridge, cool.

Follow Through

Deliver on commitments.

Think through what worked particularly well and less well to improve for the future.

Copyright © PrimeGenesis® LLC. To customize this document, download Tool 7.4 from the First-Time Leader page on www.onboardingtools.com.

ADEPT People Management

Remember, you won't get far without a committed team behind you.

An ADEPT Framework for Talent Management

Acquire

    Scope roles

    Identify prospects

Recruit and select the right people for the right roles
Attract those people
Onboard them so they can deliver better results faster

Develop
Assess performance drivers
Develop skills and knowledge for current and future roles

Encourage
Provide clear direction, objectives, measures, and so on
Support with the resources and time required for success
Recognize and reward success

Plan
Monitor people's performance over time
Assess their situation and potential
Plan career moves/succession planning over time

Transition
Migrate people to different roles to fit their needs/life stages and company needs

HOW TO HIRE GREAT PEOPLE

Adding the right people to your team in the right way is one of the most important things you do as a leader. The good news is that you're not alone. Begin by sharing your thinking with others, getting their input and deciding, together, how you are going to go forward. A good first step is crafting a complete recruiting and onboarding plan and time line. Then get important players aligned around your plan. Investment of time here makes everything else more effective and efficient down the road.

The right people can determine the future success, or failure, of your business. Many of us don't take the time to set out a structured recruiting process. As a new leader, it's imperative that you take the lead and ensure your team is on board with you. To be effective in recruiting, you must *define, develop, prepare, source, recruit, interview,* and *assess.*

Define

One of the main reasons job searches fall off track is the lack of preparation time ahead of the start.

The key to a successful search is a proper definition of the role. Thus, that is your first step. Everyone on the team should know the answers to the following questions:

- Why are we hiring?
- What strengths are absolutely required to fill this role?
- How does this role fit into our organization's vision and strategy?
- What is the value proposition of taking on the role?
- What trade-offs are we willing to take if we cannot identify and recruit the perfect star candidate?

Why Are We Hiring?

The answer to this question must be clear to everyone involved in the recruiting process—and for every role. It's important to understand why a role has become available. If it's a gap in talent, what skill(s) are you lacking within the team? If it's because someone left, be very clear as to why they left. If it's a temporary cover, what other skills would help your team move forward that you currently don't have? Understanding the reason for hiring will help the team to spot the right hire. It will also save everyone, especially you, valuable time when it gets to the interview stage.

What Strengths Are Absolutely Required to Fill This Role?

Often we do not take the required time to answer this question specifically related to the job opening at hand. It can sometimes be a challenge to nail down specifically what strengths are required to succeed in the role, especially when it's not a highly technical role.

The key is to get as specific as possible. If you are looking for a strong sales person, you would be looking for someone with excellent interpersonal, communication, and negotiation strengths. But what if we dig a little bit deeper—what kind of person tends to have those strengths? Does he or she have to come from a sales background? Not always. Think outside of the box, and put yourself in the shoes of your ideal candidate. What would you need to be successful at this role? The answers may not be obvious.

The more specific the strength, the smaller the talent pool.

How Does This Role Fit into Our Organization's Vision and Strategy?

Your role as a leader is to inspire and enable others in pursuit of a meaningful and rewarding shared purpose. Therefore it's imperative to understand how a new recruit will move the organization toward that purpose. Recruiting must be linked with overall strategy of your team and the business.

If you are a part of a start-up or a new company that has not laid out or communicated its vision, take it upon yourself to get that sorted now. It will help all involved in the business.

It can be as simple as asking

- Why are we here?
- Where do we want to go?
- How are we going to get there?

The more specific you are, the better the results.

What Is the Value Proposition of Taking on the Role?

To attract talent, you have to communicate why they should want to work for you. What's the value proposition to join your company? Why you? Why now?

It's important to market your company as much as it is to market your product or service. Google did an excellent job at doing this, and has since become one of the most desired places to work.[9] Sometimes we don't have the flexibility to offer awesome benefits like free food, but your role is to pull out the pros of working for your company.

A good place to start—Why do you work there?

What Trade-Offs Are We Willing to Take If the Star Candidate Doesn't Exist?

Before you set out on your recruiting journey, whether you are using internal or external resources, you must be clear on what you are willing to trade off.

Figure out what is needed to fill the role, and what you want from an ideal candidate. Wants are luxuries; if you find someone that possesses 90 percent of them, see it as a bonus, but don't expect it.

Communicating the wants and needs to all involved will save you time and money.

Develop a Strategy

Prepare a research strategy by answering the following nine questions:

1. In which industry or sectors is the ideal candidate currently working?
2. What are the top organization's or companies that should be targeted?
3. What job titles do the ideal candidates currently have?
4. What are the top candidates' current responsibilities?
5. From what geography should top candidates be sourced?
6. Are there any known leads or have there been any previous approaches to specific individuals for this position?
7. Which industry / professional associations could be helpful if we are to post the position?
8. Is it likely to be necessary to call in outside help to find the best candidates?
9. What is the history of filling this position?

Recruitment Methods

There are a multitude of recruitment methods available. Not all are suited for every position. Know what works for you, and what works for the different positions you are looking for.

For example, social media recruiting will not work for a highly experienced candidate, but will work great for new grads, marketers, and e-commerce candidates.

Combine a couple of methods together, and encourage out-of-the-box thinking.

In-House Recruitment Methods

If you work for an organization that already has a human resources department that takes care of recruiting, make sure you are aware of all the steps. If you don't have a human resources team, you will have to set up a base-level recruiting strategy. It's possible to integrate this with external recruiters, but we will discuss that later.

Internal Job Posting

There may be employees in other departments of your organization who are ready and qualified to move into the position. Some of the great advantages to hiring internally are

- The employee is already known.
- The culture fit is already established.
- The orientation is limited to the department, rather than the entire organization, so the adjustment period is shorter and the employee becomes productive sooner.
- The internal hire is likely to be familiar with the company's product line and possibly the customer base and industry competitors.

Looking internally should be the first step in recruiting once the position has been clearly defined.

Employee Referral

Taking into consideration that most people change jobs every three to five years, asking current employees for referrals could bring several names of appropriate potential candidates. Companies that have instituted employee referral incentive programs have found them to be quite successful. Make sure you have a system in place that enables anyone on your team meeting an exceptional person to keep track of him or her—so when you do need to hire, referrals are at the top of the pile.

External Recruitment Methods

When using an external resource, make sure that you are as specific as possible in giving direction. External recruiters do not work for your business, so do not assume you are talking the same language when describing what you are looking for. A good recruiting firm will take the time to dig deep, but you can't rely on that to happen.

Be clear on skills, years of experience, titles, career history, and what specifics you are looking for. Look for a recruiting firm that will keep you in the loop and push quality not quantity. And be patient. If you are looking for a highly skilled person, remember there are not as many on the market. Make sure you are involved with the progress of the search. Set and manage milestones. By being involved in the search, you will be able to adapt more quickly and find their runner-up.

Following are some examples of external options.

Cold calling: The old school strategy of cold calling is still a great way to reach people. If you want something, go get it. You have nothing to lose, and you never know what it can lead to. A candidate is usually always flattered to get a recruiting call, especially from the manager. He or she may not take the role, but it's a great way to network and potentially get good referrals.

The downside to cold calling is that people are becoming easier to find and harder to reach. For example, social networks like LinkedIn make it easier to connect with people out of the blue, but harder to get a response. If you do decide to go this route, keep your message simple and to the point. Do not push if the person is not interested or doesn't respond. You are representing your company, so keep it classy.

On-campus recruitment: Not only does an on-campus recruitment campaign help you fill entry-level positions, it will also give your organization exposure to candidates in future years, when they will have gained experience.

Industry associations and conferences: Associations that are specific to certain sectors, offer job referral services or postings to their membership. Some of these organizations also publish periodic newsletters.

Networking: This method can be effective with industry peers who may be able to delve into their past lives to suggest suitable candidates. Remember you can meet exceptional candidates anywhere; at a networking event, through a friend, at the gym, and so on.

Recruiting via e-mail: Short of picking up the phone, recruiting via e-mail is one of the most effective ways to get in touch with people. If you chose this method, make sure your message is clear and to the point. Don't forget to highlight your value proposition.

Internet posting: The best candidates are happy in their roles and aren't looking to change. They are known as passive candidates. Active candidates, on the other hand, are actively seeking a new role and are the ones applying to your postings.

Other external recruitment methods:

1. *Company website*
   Most companies have their own website and most of these websites include a careers section. The career site must be easy to navigate and must make the application process easy to understand and execute.

2. *Job boards*

These sites tend to be very general in nature and you can expect to receive a high volume of responses. The more generic the position, the more one would tend to use this type of recruiting method. LinkedIn, Monster, and SimplyHired are just some examples.

3. *Specialized posting sites*

There are many specialized posting sites available. They can be either industry or professional associations (such as chartered accountants or professional engineers). Some are commercial sites, specializing in a particular industry (such as oil and gas or mining). You can expect a smaller but generally better qualified response from these types of sites.

4. *LinkedIn*

LinkedIn has changed the game of recruiting. Candidates are literally at your fingertips. LinkedIn has great job posting options that are worth looking into. If you chose to make contact this way, just like with e-mail, be clear and to the point.

Social media: Social media is a great way to reach potential employees. However if done poorly it can be detrimental to your company's reputation. Make sure you have someone who is comfortable around social media; don't just give the social media responsibility to the intern. The jobs that you have posted on various sites can be linked back to your applicant tracking system. Combining this recruitment campaign with others is a great way to reach and engage your target market.

Employment agencies/search firms: For certain positions, the right agency, one that screens to your specifications, can save you a lot of time and trouble. However, are you really interviewing the best available candidates? Search firms normally boast a high find rate, sometimes at the cost of quality.

Candidate Application Process

A candidate application process ensures that no candidate gets lost. This can be integrated into a lot of today's customer relationship management software, such as Salesforce.com. If you already have an in-house system, ensure your team is using it.

Prepare

Now that you've laid out who you're looking for, how they fit into the organization, why you're filling the role, and where you're going to look, and have researched the talent pool, it's time to write the job description. Think through the following questions:

- Company description
  - Who are you?

TOOL 7.5
RECRUITMENT METHODS ANALYSIS

Position:_____ Target # of Hires:_____ By (date)_____

RECRUITMENT METHOD	HISTORY OF SUCCESS			NUMBER OF CANDIDATES IDENTIFIED/ HIRED	COST
	High	Medium	Low		
INTERNAL					
- Job Posting					
- Resumes on File					
- Employee Referrals					
EXTERNAL					
- Government Employment Center					
- Outplacement Firms					
- On-Campus Recruitment					
- Advertising					
- Professional Associations					
- Trade Journals					
- Newspapers					
- Internet (Company Website)					
- Internet (Job Posting Board)					
- Database Mining					
- Networking					
- Trade Shows					
- Professional Associations					
- Social Media					
- Open House					
- Career Exchange/Job Fair					
- Employment Agencies					
- Search Firms					
- Strategic Recruiting Firms					

- What do you do?
- What do you believe in?
- Position scope
  - Why are you hiring?
  - What purpose does the roll fill?
  - Direct reports?
- Responsibilities
  - What tasks will they carry out?
  - Who will they be managing?
  - Expectations?
  - Key Performance Indicators?
- Qualifications
  - What are the essential qualifications to successfully carry out this role (wants and needs)?
  - Education, language, certifications, experience?
- Value proposition
  - Why your company?
  - Why now?

A critical step in preparation is getting everyone aligned around what you're looking for. It's so critical, we're going to give you two different tools. The first, the Recruiting Brief, is generally useful for recruiting more senior positions. It lays out the position, mission and responsibilities, picture of success, strengths, motivation, and fit considerations. The second, the Job Requirements Checklist, may be useful for more junior positions and specifies behaviors, attributes, and skills.

TOOL 7.6
RECRUITING BRIEF

Recruit for: Job Title, Department, Compensation Grade, Start Date

Mission/responsibilities

Why position exists	
Objectives/goals/outcomes	
Impact on the rest of the organization	
Specific responsibilities	
Organizational relationships & interdependencies	

Vision (picture of success)
Strengths

Talents	
Skills (technical, interpersonal, business)	
Knowledge (education, training, experience, qualifications)	

Motivation

How activities fit with person's likes/dislikes/ideal job criteria	
How to progress towards long-term goal	

Fit

Values	
Work style, characteristics — Company's	
Work style, characteristics — Group's	
Work style, characteristics — Supervisor's	

Copyright © PrimeGenesis® LLC. To customize this document, download Tool 7.6 from the First-Time Leader page on www.onboardingtools.com.

Job Requirement Checklist

The Job Requirement Checklist contains background information that does not normally appear in the job specification but is relevant to the hiring process. Hiring is often done by a team consisting of the hiring manager, human resources, and other relevant people. It is essential that they are all on the same page when it comes to communicating the job to candidates and having a common understanding of the selection criteria.

TOOL 7.7
JOB REQUIREMENT CHECKLIST

1.1	Job Title

(continued)

1.2	Why?

1.3	When?

1.4	Target Population and Sources

1.5	Company Culture

1.6	The Package

1.7	Special Considerations

Behaviors/Attributes/Skills Checklist

		Mandatory	*Preferred*
1.	Communication		
2.	Adaptability		
3.	Reasoning/Analytical/Problem Solving		

4.	Interpersonal		
5.	Leadership		
6.	Planning and Organizational		
7.	Results/Achievements		
8.	Trainability		
9.	Judgment		
10.	Teamwork		
11.	Customer Orientation		
12.	Commitment		
13.	Creativity		
14.	Dynamism		
15.	Development		
16.	Motivation		
17.	Initiative		
18.	Accountability		
19.	Clear Thinking		
20.	Autonomy		
21.	Other (Specify)		

Source

Now it's time to make contact. Based on the recruitment methods outlined in Tool 7.5 you should have a pile of resumes on your desk to sort through. Combine a few of the methods to build your talent pool. When you spot superior talent and don't have an opening—create a role for them, because superior talent doesn't always knock on your door (especially when you really need it).

Gillian created a role for a talented individual who just had something about him she couldn't quite put her finger on. He has contributed value to the business in more ways than one, and has demonstrated skills that would not have come out in an interview. A BRAVE leader is always searching for superior talent.

TOOL 7.8
CANDIDATE SOURCING

Recruiters

Type	Names	Relationship
Internal		
External		

Direct Marketing

Category	List	Action
Personal Contacts		
Groups		
Events		

Social Networking

Site	Action
LinkedIn	
Facebook	

Advertising

Channel	Placement	Ad Creative
Web—Company Sites		
Web—Industry Sites		
Web—School Sites		
Web—Job Boards		
Print Publications		
Events		

Other

Channel	To Source	Next Step
Web		
Web		
Web		

Copyright © PrimeGenesis® LLC. To customize this document, download Tool 7.8 from the First-Time Leader page on www.onboardingtools.com.

Recruit

Depending on your role or involvement with the search process, you may not be the one making the recruiting call.

If you are making the call it is important to prepare beforehand, be in the right state of mind, and have a script ready to go.

Attract

To maximize your chances of attracting candidates when you're recruiting, you must be selling them on how great your organization is. There is no excuse for not making everyone who interviews with you want to join or refer others to you. (Candidates can sell themselves first and then do their risk assessment after they've been offered the job. Companies can't flip that switch in reverse.)

I Have Resumes. Now What?

Who should prescreen resumes?

Stop to consider who in the organization is best suited to conducting the initial screening of resumes. Factors to consider:

- Cost to organization.
- Level of understanding of the position.

How to Prescreen Resumes

If the job description contains all of the background requirements needed to do this job effectively, the screening process should be quite straightforward, putting resumes into one of three categories:

1. *Yes*—meeting key requirements including current function similar to the job you are recruiting for, key words from the job description, all the needs and most of the wants.
2. *Maybe*—having most of the needs and wants, but lacking required years of experience, and missing some technical skills (which could be trained).
3. *No*—not suitable, too many moves, missing too many needs and wants.

Unless you have expressly stated in an advertisement that you will respond only to those candidates who merit an interview, it will be necessary to respond to each and every applicant, whether or not you call them for an interview.

HELPFUL HINT

List the nonnegotiable screening parameters in front of you to consult during screening. We refer to them as the Basic Selection Criteria or Essential Screening Parameters.

Interview Candidates

We understand how being an interviewer can be as daunting as being interviewed. We've lined it all up for you, so you can feel confident and ready.

Telephone Screening Interview

A wise first step in the interview phase, as it may allow you to screen out some candidates who made it through the first "paper" screen, but do not warrant a face-to-face interview is a telephone screen. Some things that don't always come across on paper but are determinable over the phone:

- General first impressions
- Language capabilities
- Salary expectations
- Travel or mobility
- Relocation issues
- Any periods of time that are unaccounted for

The Interview Format

There are only three questions in any interview. Every question you've ever asked anyone in any interview anytime, anywhere, for any job is a subset of one of these three questions:

1. Can you do the job?
2. Will you love the job?
3. Can I stand working with you?

Or strengths, motivation, and fit. That's it. Those three. There aren't any others.

It's even easier than that. You can't really ask people if they will love the job. You can't ask people if you can stand working with them. So ask questions about their strengths, and derive answers to your other questions.[10]

- What do you need to know?
  After filling out the job brief and doing your research, you should have a good idea of what you're looking for. We've witnessed countless interviews where the interviewer asked a series of filler questions just to keep the candidate around. If you've made up your mind, don't keep him or her around. Interviews don't have a time limit.
- What not to ask
  It is your responsibility to know what questions are legal and illegal to ask. If you are heading up the recruiting process, get the information and ensure anyone interviewing is aware. The start-up world tends to be a bit more casual, which is fine. It suits the nature of their business. However, as

casual it is, it is imperative that you don't wing things that could land you in court. A lawsuit at early stages of a business is the last thing you want. Take the time to do your research and protect your organization.

To be safe, stick to job-related questions. Today, it is against the law to ask any questions relating to the following:

Age	Gender
Color	Religion
Marital status	Family status
Ethnic origin	Disability
Race	Pardoned conviction

Evaluate Fit

- Hiring for fit is more important than ever. It is often overlooked and can be difficult to assess. Poor fit is one of the main drivers of high turnover and low employee loyalty. A team of under 10 people should pay particular attention to fit. As described in Chapter 6, your company culture is what will set you apart. Learn to trust your gut. If something doesn't feel right, keep searching for someone that does. Don't settle.

GUEST EXPERT

Bill Berman's Perspective on the Importance of Cultural Fit in Hiring

Every company and every team has a culture. Organizational culture is the set of implicit or explicit rules and guidelines that explain how you should behave, communicate, and interact within the company and with customers, suppliers, and stakeholders. Hiring people who do not have a good cultural fit can create endless difficulties, and make even the most technically capable hire struggle to succeed.

In order to pick people who fit with the organizational culture, it is essential that you be able to describe what that culture is. If you can't identify your own culture, you won't be able to tell if someone will fit in that culture. Make sure, when you define the culture, you aren't describing what it *should be*—describe what it *is*. A few key questions to ask yourself about your organization include

- What is the real expectation for work hours and availability at your company? Everyone says they respect work-life balance, but

companies vary dramatically in how late people work, whether they
answer e-mails in the evening, and when they take phone calls.

- How formal/informal is your organization? I have worked with several hedge funds, none of which have more than 200 employees. Yet
  some expect all employees to wear business formal, and others are
  comfortable with jeans and polo shirts.
- How collaborative is your organization? Do different business functions work together to reach conclusions, or does each function
  operate independently? Do the regions work together, or does each
  regional head control his or her (region's profitability)? How matrixed
  is your organization? The more matrixed it is, the more you need
  people who can lead by influence and shared purpose rather than
  driving individual results.
- How flexible can you be in your company? Some businesses insist
  that their people do whatever it takes to get the job done, and others
  have clear processes and systems, and want their staff to follow those
  explicitly. Highly flexible people will struggle with an organization
  that is process driven, and process-driven individuals will founder in
  highly flexible companies.

If you have trouble defining your own culture, there are lots of tests on the
market that can help you describe the culture. Better yet, sit down with
your team and ask them to write single-word adjectives on 3x5 cards that
describe the organization as it is and as you would like it to be. Then take
the cards and define your culture.

Once you know your culture, make sure your recruitment process
examines individuals' style and cultural preferences as well as their skill
level. Aside from the few critical skills that are essential to the job on entry,
people with a good cultural fit will learn and adapt to the new role better
than people whose values and expectations differ from your organization.

When you put together your prospect candidate campaign, test every
message and channel decision against cultural fit. Keep it simple. Just chart
messages and channels on a skill match/culture match grid. Messages and
channels that have a high match for skills and a high match for culture are,
obviously, your best bets.[11]

	Low Culture Match	High Culture Match
High Skill Match	Tempting Could yield people who do more harm than good	Best
Low Skill Match	Worst	Easy to overlook Could yield people who can grow into job

TOOL 7.9
INTERVIEW GUIDE

Candidate:
Position (grade):
Key communication points about organization:

Strength #1:
Question

Data

Rating_____ (1: no evidence; 2: evidence does not support hire; 3: hirable;
4: strong; 5: outstanding)

Strength #2:
Question

Data

Rating_____ (1: no evidence; 2: evidence does not support hire; 3: hirable;
4: strong; 5: outstanding)

Strength #3
Question

Data

Rating_____ (1: no evidence; 2: evidence does not support hire; 3: hirable;
4: strong; 5: outstanding)

Assess

Assess multiple candidates in bulk, versus individually. This allows for benchmarking. In doing this, take good notes during the interviews so that you can remember the answer that was given to each question. Rate the answers 1 to 5, or A to F, or something else.

Whichever rating system you use, communicate it clearly to each member of the team. There will always be a disparity between one person's rating and another, but the effects of this can be minimized by having a common rating system.

Some questions are more critical than others, and these should be weighted accordingly when assessing the candidates against each other.

Assessment Tools

There are many assessment tools on the market. They measure personality, strengths, weaknesses, management styles, communication style, and so on. They can be great assets when assessing multiple candidates, but they are not meant to be decision makers. Do not base hires on assessment results. Use them to build on your assumptions and what you know of the candidate. They can be great starting points for employee development.

Reference checks: Depending on where you are located and the prevailing privacy legislation, you may or may not have to get the candidate's permission to contact references. If it is required in your jurisdiction, it is your job to get a form completed with the candidate's signature.

TOOL 7.10
INTERVIEW DEBRIEF FORM

Rating (1: no evidence; 2: evidence does not support hire; 3: hirable; 4: strong; 5: outstanding)

Candidate	Strength 1	Strength 2	Strength 3	Motivation	Fit
Comments/Action					

Copyright © PrimeGenesis® LLC. To customize this document, download Tool 7.10 from the First-Time Leader page on www.onboardingtools.com.

TOOL 7.11
REFERENCE INQUIRY
AUTHORIZATION FORM

Name of Candidate: _____

I hereby authorize _____ to take references from the following
_____ (#) individuals:

NAME	ORGANIZATION	PHONE NUMBER

Signature of Candidate: _____

Date: _____

Reference inquiry: The ideal referees are former bosses, colleagues, and/or subordinates of the candidates you are considering. Personal references are considered to be of little value.

When you are contacting the referees make sure you do so with discretion. Follow the reference inquiry form in Tool 7.12, customized for the position.

TOOL 7.12
REFERENCE INQUIRY

Candidate:

Client: **Position:**

Date:

By:

Reference Person:

Person Called: Position:

Company: Phone Number:

A. Opening

    1. What was relationship with reference to candidate?

    Relationship: (from   to   )

B. Work and Business Experience

    1. Technical expertise and conceptual ability

        How would you describe his/her technical knowledge and ability?

        What new innovation did he/she introduce to implement change in the organization?

    2. Tactical skills

        How would you describe his/her administrative ability?

        How would you describe his/her organizational ability?

        Is he/she effective at recognizing and solving difficult situations?

        Would you say he/she has good judgment (business and personal)?

        Is he/she sensitive to the reaction of others?

        Is he/she flexible?

        Is he/she objective?

    3. Supervision development

        Describe his/her work habits:

- Ability to manage his/her own time
- Ability to deal with details and routine
- Reliability and dependability

        How would you compare him/her with other people at his level?

- Problem solving
- Initiative and/or drive
- Analytical ability
- Imagination
- Creativity
- Follow-through
- Growth potential

(continued)

Is he/she more of a doer or a delegator?

- Describe his/her leadership ability
- Describe his/her ability to work under pressure (energy level)
- How does he/she go about making decisions?
- Does he/she respect timetables and deadlines?
- Does he/she deliver on commitments?

4. Communication skills

Describe how he/she supervises and/or handles people (including methods of supervision):

- People superior to him/her
- At his/her own level
- Below him/her
- Clients/suppliers
- Ability to motivate
- Ability to delegate
- Describe his/her effectiveness in speaking/writing:
- Is he/she bilingual? (mandate specific)
- Describe his/her public speaking ability:

- Describe his/her ability to listen:

5. Motivation/career expectations

Has he/she had a stable career?

Would you describe him/her as:
- Ethical
- Discreet
- Loyal
- Self-confident
- Mature

6. Miscellaneous

What are his/her three outstanding strengths?

Recognizing that we all have shortcomings, what areas do you see where further development could help him/her be a more effective performer?

If you were to recommend anything to improve this individual's management skills, what type of support would you recommend?

Would you reemploy him/her or like to work with him/her again?

How would you describe his/her personality? (i.e., aggressiveness, self-confidence, etc.)

Plus factors:

Areas for improvement:

C. Conclusion
    1. Do you have any other recommendations or reservations?

Additional comments:

Copyright © Alan Davis & Associates Inc. To customize this document, download Tool 7.12 from the First-Time Leader page on www.onboardingtools.com.

If you have followed the process it will be rare that you get a bad reference. However, if you do, it is incumbent upon you not to ignore it and to investigate further. Some candidates are masterful at passing interviews and representing someone who is not really themselves. The reference check is the last gate before the offer.

If you have followed the guidelines, your top choices should be obvious. Yet it always helps to get a second opinion. So get one if you can—especially from your human resources department if your company has one.

Making the Offer

If you are the decision maker, now is the time to make the job offer. Tool 7.13 will help. The key point is that this is a strategic sale that should be made only if the match is right for the offeree. Give offerees a chance to think through and talk through their concerns with others before accepting.

BRINGING NEW HIRES INTO THE TEAM

Put your new recruits on the road to success even before they start. Make them feel welcome and valuable to an organization they can take pride in. Ensure that each new employee has a BRAVE onboarding plan in place. Encourage and enable relationships and provide new recruits with any help they may need along the way.

Prepare Your Own Message and Touch Point Plan

Start with your own message to new recruits. What do you want them to understand, believe, and do? These might include the context of their role, your vision

TOOL 7.13
OFFER CLOSING PROCESS

Candidate:

Position:

Key Influencers:

Why organization and role are right for candidate (overlap with needs, hopes, and desires):

Why candidate is right for organization and role:

Candidate's concerns:

Key influencers' needs, hopes, desires and concerns:

Ways to alleviate concerns:

Verbal offer made (by whom, when):

Written offer delivered (by whom, when):

Assistance with due diligence—items for follow-up action:

Calls:

Other live meetings to alleviate concerns and drive messages about organization, role, candidate:

Target acceptance date:

of success for them, your ideas around their priorities, what resources they can tap to drive success, and a call to action.

Craft a plan to deliver that message. Manage the welcoming signs and symbols—especially your own time. Model the behaviors and attitudes that you want your new recruits to adopt. Preempt others' potentially counterproductive influences on the new recruits by telling them stories in advance about the organization that help them understand it.

Follow through with your own media/touch point plan. Think about things like prestart meetings, calls, notes, and packages. Just don't disappear until day 1. If possible, be there to welcome new recruits and introduce them on day 1. Investing time in your recruits will help them understand and believe how much you value them.

TOOL 7.14
ANNOUNCEMENT CASCADE

1. **Stakeholders** (internal and external)
   Emotionally impacted:

   Directly impacted:

   Indirectly impacted:

   Less impacted:

2. **Message**
   Platform for change:　　　　　　　　Headline:

   Vision:　　　　　　　　　　　　　　Message Points:

   Call to action:

3. **Pre-announcement Time Line** (one-on-ones, small groups, large groups)
   Prior to announcement day
   　　One-on-one:

   Announcement day
   　　One-on-one:

   (continued)

> Small groups:
>
> **4. Formal Announcement**
>   Method: _____
>   Timing: _____
>
> **5. Post-announcement Time Line** (one-on-ones, small groups, large
>   groups, mass)
>   One-on-one:
>
>   Small groups:
>
>   Large groups:
>

Encourage and Enable Relationships

As you know, one of the big things new recruits can do between acceptance and their first day on the job is to jump-start key relationships. You can and should help your recruits identify the most important stakeholders that they should connect with before their first day. Make the introductions. Then get out of the way.

If the position has been open for a long time, you've probably been doing at least part of your new recruit's job. Along the way, you've established relationships with people who are going to be working closely with the new recruit. There is a risk that the strength of your relationships with these people can get in the way of your new recruit's building his or her own relationships with them. Take a step back as necessary so you don't undermine your new recruit's communication or decision flows with those key people. We're not in any way suggesting that you ignore or damage these key relationships. Just allow them to adjust to the new situation.

Provide Help

There's no doubt in our completely unbiased minds that giving this book to the people you hire is a great way to help them succeed. The question is when? Giving this book to them the day after they accept the job will allow them to take advantage of the fuzzy front end (between acceptance and day 1). It would be even better to give them a copy when they receive the offer to help them better assess the risks they are facing and prepare for their new roles. You really do want them to know and understand the risks. You and your organization will be far better off if your recruits turn down the job, than if they accept a bad match, show up, and fail.

Since we wrote the first edition of *The New Leader's 100-Day Action Plan*, an entire industry has grown up around executive onboarding. Most of the practitioners focus on assimilation coaching, helping new leaders assimilate into their new culture. This is a vital service, but it is not the only assistance that can benefit new leaders. Think in terms of helping your new recruits on three levels: accommodating, assimilating, and accelerating.

Accommodating is all about providing resources to help them get set up in their office and at home—particularly if they are moving. The office part would include desks, computers, phones, passwords, and so on. This is relatively straightforward stuff. Just make sure someone is taking care of the things laid out in Tool 7.15, the Accommodation Checklist.

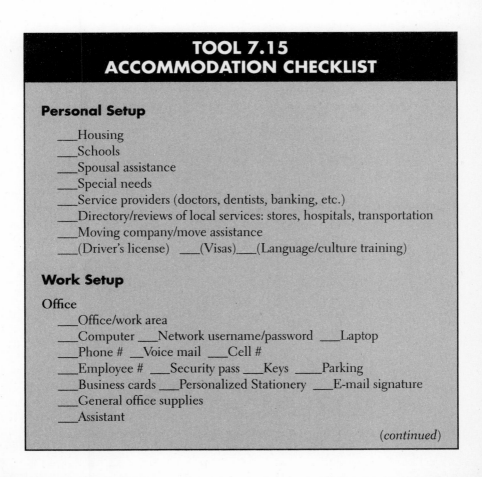

TOOL 7.15
ACCOMMODATION CHECKLIST

Personal Setup

____Housing
____Schools
____Spousal assistance
____Special needs
____Service providers (doctors, dentists, banking, etc.)
____Directory/reviews of local services: stores, hospitals, transportation
____Moving company/move assistance
____(Driver's license) ____(Visas)____(Language/culture training)

Work Setup

Office
____Office/work area
____Computer ____Network username/password ____Laptop
____Phone # __Voice mail ____Cell #
____Employee # ____Security pass ____Keys ____Parking
____Business cards ____Personalized Stationery ____E-mail signature
____General office supplies
____Assistant

(continued)

Information
___Where to go for information (intranet, bulletin boards, etc.)
___Organization history
___Business plans
___Financials
___Organizational charts
___Job descriptions and appraisals of direct reports
___Organization directory with names, photos, job titles, contact info
___Facility addresses, contacts, travel directions
___Glossary of organization specific terms
___Customers ___Collaborators ___Capabilities ___Competitors
___Conditions

Transition Assistance
___Spotlight profile on intranet, other open-access locations
___Orientation
___"How we do things around here" buddy
___Mentor/coach or ____Transition accelerator

Copyright © PrimeGenesis® LLC. To customize this document, download Tool 7.15 from the First-Time Leader page on www.onboardingtools.com.

Assimilating is the next level up. Here you can help them map their stakeholders and make sure that they have orientation and onboarding programs and meetings set up, and also have the time to follow through on them per Tool 7.16, the Assimilation Checklist.

TOOL 7.16
ASSIMILATION CHECKLIST

Introduction to key stakeholders for onboarding conversations (up, across, down; internal, external; information providers, resource controllers; suppliers, customers; cross-hierarchy, cross-function, cross-region)

Introduction to informal, behind-the-scenes networks like sports teams, communities of common interest, and so on

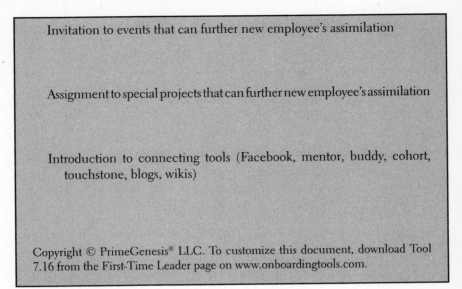

Invitation to events that can further new employee's assimilation

Assignment to special projects that can further new employee's assimilation

Introduction to connecting tools (Facebook, mentor, buddy, cohort, touchstone, blogs, wikis)

Accelerating is one more level up. Not every new recruit needs to accelerate his or her onboarding. Acceleration is not appropriate when the person you hire has a lot of time to learn and the risk of doing something wrong outweighs the risk of not doing something right. But when there is a need for a new person and his or her team to deliver better results faster, acceleration is essential. In that scenario help the new hire follow the program in this book. Better yet, consider bringing in people with an expertise in this process to give him or her extra leverage up front. It will all but guarantee that the new hire and his or her team deliver better results faster.

TOOL 7.17
ACCELERATION CHECKLIST

Imperative—Resources available for new employee to get imperative in place by day 30

Milestones—Resources available for new employee to get milestone management process in place by day 45

Early wins—Help employee select early win by day 60

(continued)

Role sort—Encourage employee to think through role sort by day 70

Communication—Resources available to support employee's communication plan

Copyright © PrimeGenesis® LLC. To customize this document, download Tool 7.17 from the First-Time Leader page on www.onboardingtools.com.

Michael Moniz—Onboarding as a Crucible of Leadership[12]

How people manage onboarding leaves a lasting impact on all involved. It is a crucible of leadership—a transformational experience that helps shape all involved. During the first 100 days of a new job, the journey and the relationships built are just as important as the end point.

Whether you are a new leader yourself or are helping a new leader transition into a new job or assignment, give executive onboarding the attention it deserves by thinking in terms of destination, context, and communication.

Step One: Destination

> After two months, we reached the very top of Everest. It was pitch black. I was hypoxic. At −50 degrees Fahrenheit, my camera froze after two shots. We needed to get down quickly. . . .
>
> It was not about the experience on the top of the world. It was about the journey and the relationships . . . the lasting, enduring memories, experiences and moments we suffered through and enjoyed together.

This story was told to George by Michael Moniz, avid alpine climber and CEO of Circadence, as he explored the parallels between executive onboarding and mountain climbing.

Circadence designs and builds technologies for delivering data across networks of all types. To best take advantage of the remarkable adoption rate of smartphones and tablets and the tremendous increase in mobile network traffic, the company brought on Gary Morton as SVP (Senior Vice President) of engineering to lead development of its new mobile platforms.

Like a first mountain ascent, those tackling a new market "have to be excited about challenging the impossible," Moniz said. His new SVP had the strengths required for the role and seemed to fit with the team so the focus was making sure he had a real burning desire to tackle the challenge.

Destination: Commit to the cause yourself, or help people you bring in understand and commit to the cause.

Step Two: Context

Before even getting to a mountain, Moniz studies the terrain and the weather, and looks for patterns in others' successes or failures. Then he chooses the team, route, and resources appropriate for the context.

New SVP Morton faced similar challenges in building Circadence's mobile solutions. He had to pull together a team from a limited global pool of talent. Of the infinite possibilities, Morton had to pick the most promising route/architecture for the new solutions. And he had to get the right balance of resources—neither too few nor too many at any moment.

Context: Choose the team, route, and resources appropriate for the context.

Step Three: Communication

The most successful mountaineers and businesspeople constantly think through scenarios and options, looking for different ways through the next crevasse field.

Just as Moniz and his Sherpa, Chewang Lindu, are literally tethered together by their climbs, he and his new SVP had to partner for success. They spent time together both in and outside the office (including a long winter climb) until the new SVP's belief in Moniz and understanding of his vision gave him—according to Moniz—a "platform of confidence to build his team."

Moniz built on that platform, giving his new SVP

- The latitude and *resources* to execute
- Realistic *boundaries* so he could operate safely for himself and the team
- Assistance in bridging *relationships* across the entire team

Communication: Follow through in terms of adjusting resources, boundaries, and relationships.

Results

New leaders fail because of poor fit, poor delivery, or an inability to adjust to surprises. Moniz said that his new SVP is now "comfortable coming to me with breakthroughs and issues." He fits. He has delivered a new generation of technology and applications that have resulted in new customers. He has adjusted to surprises—including losing a key senior engineer and going through personal challenges. He has become adept at triaging product marketing and sales requests by focusing all on what's really essential. It's a great example of coming through the leadership crucible of onboarding well.

> ⛵
>
> Implications for you: The basics matter, no matter how high the peak.

MANAGING PEOPLE WHO ARE DOING WELL—AND NOT SO WELL

You have to do both. You have to develop both the strong and the less strong.

Develop (the *D* in ADEPT People Management)

Identify the most important drivers of performance, assess how individuals are doing against them, and then develop their skills and knowledge in those areas.

As a leader you will want to strengthen people's skills and knowledge to help them be more successful in their current role and prepare them for future roles.

We agree with Gallup's notion that a strength is a combination of talents, skills, and knowledge. Since talent is innate, you can't do anything to build that. So your focus should be on skills and knowledge. We also agree with Gallup that your focus should be on helping people get even stronger in areas of strength rather than trying to develop their weaknesses into strengths. That process will be frustrating for everyone involved. It is far better to build on their strengths, and help them mitigate their weaknesses in other ways.[13]

Career Planning Tool and Discussion

Some of you are probably wondering why we're kicking off the Develop section of ADEPT with career planning. You might think it belongs under Plan. You would be right if we were talking about organizational planning. We're not. We're talking about developing individuals. And, in the spirit of Steven Covey, we're going to "begin with the end in mind."[14] This is a great exercise to run with the people on your team once a year or so.

1. Likes and dislikes
   Have them lay out what they particularly like and dislike across activities, jobs, situations, lifestyle, and anything else they want to talk about. This is your raw data.
2. Ideal job criteria
   Have them look at their ideal job criteria across the dimensions of good for others, good for me, and good at it. These include impact on others, match

with personal values, influence on the organization in terms of good for others; enjoyable work/activities, fit with life interests, reward, recognition, respect in terms of good for me; match between activities and strengths, learning, development, and resume building in terms of good at it. They should also think about their life interests.

3. Long-term goals
Separately, they should lay out their long-term goals. These could be three-year, five-year, lifetime, or whatever. It doesn't matter—whatever they are most comfortable with. Once they've completed these three tasks, they should meet with you.

4. Options
At that meeting, think through options together—both within and outside the organization. Remember, this is an exercise in helping them create their long-term plan, not pushing them in a direction you think is right for them. Having thought the options through, they need to make their plans real.

5. Choice
Having created a range of options, they can make their choices by evaluating the options created against their ideal job criteria and long-term goals.

6. Gut check
But, before anyone does anything, they should sleep on their choices and see how they feel in the morning. If they wake up feeling good, move forward. If they wake up with something gnawing at their gut, they lied to themselves—probably about the weight they put on the different elements of their ideal job criteria. Push them to recalibrate, rethink, and choose again until it feels right. (It's okay to lie to yourself if you have a mechanism in place to catch it.)

Development Plans

Development plans are all about helping people develop. The trap is that some managers focus development plans exclusively on fixing problems. We think it's better to help people further develop their strengths (as well as fixing some problems).

In that light are the following 10 steps.

1. Select the areas for development.
2. Lay out a developmental goal for the period (generally one year).
3. Work out a developmental approach and plan.
4. Be explicit about the resources to be deployed including money, personnel, and time.

TOOL 7.18
CAREER PLANNING

1. List your likes and dislikes
   Activities:
   Jobs:
   Situations:
   Lifestyle:
   Other:

2. List your ideal job criteria categorized as follows:
   Good for others (impact on others, match with personal values, influence on organization):

   Good for me (enjoyable work/activities, fit with life interests, reward, recognition, respect):

   Good at it (match between activities and strengths, learning, development, resume builder):

   Life interests (application of technology, quantitative analysis, theory development, conceptual thinking, creative production, counseling and mentoring, managing people and relationships, enterprise control, influence through language and ideas):

3. Identify your long-term goals.

4. Build a broad range of options that meet your long-term goals.

5. Make choices by evaluating your options against your criteria.

Finally, perform a gut check.

5. Clarify the responsibilities of person being developed.
6. Agree on the responsibilities of the manager/coach—generally you.
7. Agree on timing and the milestones along the way.
8. Implement.
9. Monitor and track.
10. Adjust as appropriate.

TOOL 7.19
DEVELOPMENT PLAN

Development plans are all about helping people develop. The trap is that some managers focus development plans exclusively on fixing problems. We think it's better to help people further develop their strengths (as well as fixing some problems). Do this for each element:

Area for development:

Developmental goal for the period:

Developmental approach/plan:

Resources to be deployed:

Responsibilities of person being developed:

Responsibilities of manager/coach:

Timing/milestones:

Encourage (the *E* in ADEPT People Management)

Whoever taught you to say "please" and "thank you" was prescient. This is the key to encouraging people on your team.

Please is all about clarity around expectations: objectives, goals, and measures. It's about enabling people to succeed by making sure they have the direction, resources, tools, and support they need and then getting out of their way. (And getting others out of their way.)

Thank you is about providing the recognition and rewards that encourage each individual. Multiple studies have shown that, in general, people are positively motivated by things like the type of work they are doing, challenge and achievement, promotion prospects, responsibility, and recognition or esteem. Things like salary, relationship with colleagues, working conditions, and their supervisor's style are basic factors that don't motivate if they are in the acceptable range, but can quickly demotivate if there is a problem.

So the general prescription isn't all that hard. Make sure the basic factors are good enough and won't cause problems, and invest in the real motivators. It is not about motivating people. It is about enabling people to succeed so they can tap into their own inner motivations. Seek to enable your team.

You can encourage people by

Clarifying how their individual roles fit with the broader group.

Establishing individual SMART goals for them.

Goal Setting

John Michael Loh, United States Air Force Air Combat Command during the first Gulf War said, "I used to believe that if it doesn't get measured, it doesn't get done. Now I say if it doesn't get measured it doesn't get approved . . . you need to manage by facts, not gut feel."

George Doran created an acronym for thinking about goals: SMART—Specific, Measurable, Actionable/Attainable, Relevant, Time bound.[15]

In brief, goals work when they are

Specific—Concrete objectives are easier to achieve and track.

Measurable—If you can't measure it, you can't manage it.

Actionable/Attainable—Things we can make happen or influence (and achieve).

Relevant—To our overall mission, strategy, plan.

Time bound—Including milestones along the way.

If an eight-year-old can't tell if the goal was achieved or not at the end of the period, it's not SMART enough.

TOOL 7.20
SMART GOALS

SMART: *Specific, Measurable, Actionable/Attainable, Relevant, Time bound*
  Specific—Concrete objectives are easier to achieve and track.
  Measurable—If you can't measure it, you can't manage it.
  Actionable/Attainable—Things we can make happen or influence (and achieve).
  Relevant—To our overall mission, strategy, plan.
  Time bound—Including milestones along the way.

To customize this document, download Tool 7.20 from the First-Time Leader page on www.onboardingtools.com.

Team Charter   Goals work for individuals and teams. For project-focused teams, it's also useful to give them a charter. This should include

Objectives/Goals—Clarify what specific, measurable results (SMART) they are asked to deliver.

Context—Provide the information that led to the objectives/goals you gave them. A part of this is the intent behind the objectives so they know how their output will impact others and what will happen after the objective is achieved.

Resources—Explain the human, financial, and operational resources available to the team. Also make them aware of other teams, groups, units working in parallel, supporting, or interdependent areas.

Guidelines—Clarify what the team can and cannot do with regard to roles and decisions. Lay out the interdependencies between the team being chartered and the other teams involved.

Accountability—Be clear on accountability structure, update timing, completion timing.

Required Resources   Just as it is important for people to understand how their goals fit with the rest of the organization, it is equally important to make sure that people have the resources and support (internally and externally) they need to achieve their goals. It would be silly to ask the sales force to sell 100 widgets per day with plant capacity of 50 per day. You would end up with unhappy customers, furious salespeople, and nervous breakdowns throughout the plant.

To help reinforce the creation, deployment, and achievement of goals, you need assistance. That assistance comes in the form of seven reinforcements:

TOOL 7.21
TEAM CHARTER

Useful for getting teams off to the best start.

Objectives/Goals: Charge the team with delivering specific, measurable results (SMART).

Context:
Information that led to objectives:

Intent behind the objectives:

What's going to happen after the objective is achieved:

Resources: Human, financial, and operational resources available to the team. Other teams, groups, units working in parallel, supporting, or interdependent areas.

Guidelines: Clarify what the team can and cannot do with regard to roles and decisions. Lay out the interdependencies between the team being chartered and the other teams involved.

Accountability: Be clear on accountability structure, update timing, completion timing.

Copyright © PrimeGenesis® LLC. To customize this document, download Tool 7.21 from the First-Time Leader page on www.onboardingtools.com.

skills, knowledge, tools, resources, guidelines, linking performance and consequences, and driving actions and milestones along the way.

1. **Skills:** These are the how-to's or capabilities. Your goals may be perfect, but you will not reach them without the necessary skills in place. Know what those skills are, and know which ones you have to develop.
2. **Knowledge:** This boils down to facts that you are aware of and your experiences. The greater your breadth and depth of knowledge, the higher your chance of reaching your goals.
3. **Tools:** Without the right equipment, you cannot reach your goals. You must know what equipment is needed, what you have, and how to fill the gap.

4. **Resources:** The three key resource needs are human, financial, and operational. Make sure that resources are available to support your established goals in each of these areas. If not, you either have to change your goals to make them more realistic, or increase your access to the needed resource.

5. **Guidelines:** Establish boundaries so that everyone knows how far they can run. Everyone should know the things that you cannot do because they are outside the clearly established guidelines.

6. **Link between performance and consequences:** Make the link between performance and consequences explicit. If that link is properly established, everyone should know how the results will be rated. As many organizations get larger and more bureaucratic, they tend to bunch people's annual raises in a narrow range, doing things like giving those who meet expectations a 3 percent to 5 percent raise and those who exceed a 4 percent to 6 percent raise. Over time, this has a devastating effect on performance because people see that they are not going to be rewarded for putting in extra effort to over deliver and won't get punished for marginal under delivery.

7. **Actions and milestones along the way:** You cannot do midcourse corrections if you do not know where you're supposed to be at midcourse. It is far easier to spot a problem when someone says, "We produced 9 widgets last month versus a goal of 30" than when someone says, "We experienced normal start-up issues but remain fully committed to producing 360 widgets this year."

People Management

The basic concept here is that on-the-spot feedback can save you all sorts of time and angst over the long term and earn you respect. Tool 7.22 is George's cheat sheet to a couple of useful techniques.

The overriding idea is to notice and react to events. When you notice one, start by clarifying what happened and why. It may be helpful to confirm what you think you saw. Then make a choice. If this is something you need to change, drop into criticizing or managing differences mode. If this is something you want to encourage, drop into crediting or building mode.

Constructive Criticism

If you choose to criticize, it's generally best to itemize the merits (things you value) and concerns. Discuss these with the person involved, trying to find a way to retain the merits and eliminate the concerns.

Suzi, love your blouse. Not sure it goes with the really short cut-off jeans. Perhaps you can find something else that will go even better with the blouse.

Managing Differences

This happens when the person you're trying to influence sees things totally differently than you do. The prescription here is to explore the differences. Try to zero in on what's really important. Then find ways to alter the restrictions. Explore some alternatives. If you can't agree, end the conversation.

> "But I love my cut-offs."
> "They look great. Just not in the office."
> "But I love them."
> "Could you wear them to and from the office and change into something different while you're here?"
> "That would be a hassle."
> "Okay then. I'm going to outvote you. No more cut-offs in the office."

Credit

This is the fun stuff. Any time you can pat someone on the back is a good time— providing it's real. People see through gratuitous praise. This simple formula forces you to think through what and why you're crediting for and makes it real to the person being praised.

1. Make a general reference to the area you're crediting: "Nice job with that new customer yesterday."
2. Make a specific reference to what the individual did: "The way you established rapport by referencing your shared interest in Wallyball was wonderful."
3. Note the personal qualities that helped the person do what he or she did: "It's another example of how your thoroughness in preparing for meetings pays off."
4. Close with the resulting benefits to the organization and person: "By the way, your work was a huge contributor to us closing the sale this morning. You're getting the commission."

Building

Building is another good news communication—if done right. This is one that can wrong very quickly.

1. Start by acknowledging the connection to the original idea: "Love your idea about a team lunch tomorrow to help us bond."
2. Add value by modifying, adding benefits, bringing in other applications, or coming up with new ways to realize the original intent: "We could invite some of our allies as well."
3. Be careful not to change the idea in a way that destroys the original intent: "Instead of a lunch, perhaps you can all come to my office at the end of the day to see the slides from my recent trip to WallaWalla."

4. Finally, check back with the idea owner to make sure you've preserved his or her idea (back to inviting allies): "Do you think the addition of allies would be a good thing or would it dilute the core team's bonding?"

TOOL 7.22
PEOPLE MANAGEMENT TOOLS

Event:	Clarify what, why Confirm Change—criticize, manage differences Maintain—credit, build
Clarify and confirm	Additional information about what and why
Constructive criticism	1. Itemize merits and concerns 2. Discuss how to retain merits and eliminate concerns 3. Summarize
Managing differences	1. Explore difference—what's important? How to alter restrictions 2. Explore alternatives 3. End the conversation—it's okay to decide differently
Credit	1. General reference to area crediting 2. Specific reference to what individual did 3. Personal qualities that helped person do what he or she did 4. Resulting benefits to organization and person
Building	1. Acknowledge connection 2. Add value—modify, add benefits, other applications, new ways to realize original intent 3. Check back with idea owner to make sure you've preserved his or her idea

To customize this document, download Tool 7.22 from the First-Time Leader page on www.onboardingtools.com.

Managing Behavior

George attended a workshop on managing behavior by Paul Brown a couple of decades ago. Paul's basic model has stuck with George, and he's been using it ever since.

1. **Pinpoint** the specific behavior to be changed. But before you do anything, ask yourself if it is legitimate to push the person to change. It is if the behavior is impacting either (a) the individual's output, (b) others' output, or (c) the individual's future career.

    For example, if the individual always wears orange and black shirts and you know that a senior executive has a completely irrational hatred of anything that reminds him of Princeton University (whose colors are orange and black), you might suggest a change in color scheme even though it has no real impact on output.

2. **Track** occurrences of the behavior and decide if it's worth the effort to change it. If it happens once in a blue moon (a month in which there are

TOOL 7.23
MANAGING BEHAVIOR

Pinpoint	Specific behavior to be changed Question whether it's legitimate to push the change: • Is it impacting the individual's output? • Is it impacting others' output? • Is it impacting the individual's future career?
Track	Quantify occurrences of behavior • Worth the effort to change?
Analyze	• Antecedents • Consequences—balance of consequences • Behavior
Change	The environment • Antecedents • Consequences
Evaluate	By comparing to baseline

To customize this document, download Tool 7.23 from the First-Time Leader page on www.onboardingtools.com.

two full moons) then don't worry. If it happens 31 times a day, that's a different story.

3. **Analyze** the ABCs: Antecedents, Behavior, Consequences and balance of consequences.
4. **Change the environment** by either prompting new behavior (antecedent) or changing the balance of consequences so there are more negative and fewer positive consequences of undesired behavior and more positive and fewer negative consequences of desired behavior.
5. **Evaluate** by comparing the new behaviors to your baseline.

The key to this whole thing is changing the balance of consequences — and often reducing the positive consequences of undesired behavior.

Transformational change requires aligning plans, people, and practices around a shared purpose. Tackling those pieces with the right approach and resources step-by-step in stages instead of all at once is often the difference between success and failure. Do four things:

1. Align plans, people, and practices around a shared purpose.
2. Manage the transition in stages with different approaches and resources at each stage as appropriate.
3. Jettison each stage's excess baggage before it gets in the way of the next stage's success.
4. Celebrate your early successes.

Case Study: Building Communication Satellites[16]

Brent Stoute and his team build things that cannot fail. Each component of their communication satellites has to work for 15 years with no maintenance, no tune-ups, no failures, no questions asked. Building a satellite to this standard of quality is a gargantuan task, best managed in digestible chunks.

When George spoke with Stoute about this, he told George about one organization that wanted to hire his company, MDA, to design and build a satellite payload for it. The twist was that the company wanted to have a team of its engineers shadow Stoute's group so they could learn how to design and build their own satellite payloads after the first one.

Stoute encouraged the company to have its engineers engage with one part of the operation first, learn that, practice that, and then learn another part and another part. "Why try to digest the whole meal at once?" he argued. Further, it's not enough for an organization's people to learn the skills. The company needs to have plans and practices in place to complete the transformation successfully.

Plans

Big, audacious space or terrestrial missions are inspiring. The trap is thinking that just declaring the mission is enough. Helping the world communicate better, feeding the poor, saving the world from disease does not happen without well thought through strategy and plans.

People

Transformations, as discussed here, involve leveraging existing capabilities to grow in new areas. Numerous opportunities surface for existing employees to fill these newly created roles; however, one must consider how the baseline work will be maintained.

It's essential to know what talents, knowledge, and skills you're going to need at different stages of a transformation, how you're going to get them in place when you need them, and how you're going to transition them to other roles or organizations when they have completed their transformational tasks. Know which people you can develop, which you can recruit, and which you're going to have to bring in with acquisitions as part of capability step changes.

Never forget that maintaining existing employee morale is a key element, and the decisions regarding new assignments should not be taken lightly. The amount of energy released from a well-motivated employee can make the difference between transformation success and failure.

As expected, a balanced approach between existing and new employee assignments should yield optimum results for such exciting initiatives. Further, the onboarding process is also a key element in the rapid formation of a cohesive team.

Practices

Even with the most compelling purpose, winning plans, and the right people, major transformations don't stick until they are embedded in the systems and culture. Be clear on what changes you are making related to the firm's behaviors, relationships, attitudes, values, and environment, per the BRAVE culture model.

Be clear on how you're going to manage the steps to get there. Sometimes you can manage the change from within. Sometimes you'll need the catalyst of an acquisition or merger to drive a cultural step change. Additionally, never forget the power of early successes to sustain momentum. Early wins also help motivate the team, which can carry it through difficult times, should they occur.

Utilize the Right Resources by Stage

Just like mission control jettisons the first stage of a rocket when its job is done, just like a baseball manager pulls the middle relief pitcher when it's time for the closer, do not shy away from the stage-by-stage step changes to people and practices required to deliver your transformation. Major transformations require tough choices at every step of the way.

Implications for you: Break complex initiatives into stages.

Performance Assessment

It's highly useful to assess performance at the end of the period in order to make sure you keep doing what works and improve what needs to be improved.

We believe in the value of results. Start with results versus objectives. If you've got SMART goals in place these should be self-evident.

Then look at learnings and accomplishments: What worked? What needs to improve? What was learned about self?

Take a look at strengths and gaps and career interests (if you haven't put in place an up-to-date career plan).

Use those to set new objectives.

Performance assessments are an excellent time to drive the overall business goals.

Gillian knew that excellent candidate follow-up made their recruiting business outperform their competitors. However, she had a challenge getting her team members to spend time on what they considered to be a menial task—that is, it didn't fit into the completion of finishing a mandate. Although she pushed how important it was, giving examples, it never really clicked.

Finally, she took the opportunity at each individual's midyear review to explain how candidate management done correctly leads to new business, good candidates, and good word-of-mouth referrals, helping the overall state of the business. Conversely, by not conducting this task, they were losing out to their competitors.

Gillian saw the lights bulbs switch on immediately. Even though she had rattled on about this many times over in meetings, she had never tied it to how this small menial task affected the overall state of the business. Since then, she tries to explain the Why? in as much detail as possible. Now, once everyone understands how their roles impact the business, they buy in and energy increases.

TOOL 7.24
PERFORMANCE ASSESSMENT

Results versus objectives:

(continued)

Learnings and accomplishments:

What worked:

What needs to improve:

What learned about self:

Strengths:

Gaps:

Career interests:

New objectives:

Plan (The *P* in ADEPT People Management)

Good planning starts with a situational and opportunity assessment. Organizational planning is closely linked with strategic planning. Figure out where you're going and the choices you will implement to get there. Then map out the organization, starting with what it needs to look like in the future state. Armed with that, you can look at people's performance to assess where they are now, where they could get to, and how they can best fit into the future organization.

The organizational evolution curve is hard to stay ahead of. A little long-term planning can go a long way. Make the mental jump to the organization of the future. Then step back and figure out what you have to do to get there. Some people can grow into their new roles by doing what they're doing now. Some people can grow into their new roles with an investment in their skills and knowledge. Some people can't grow into the roles and will have to be guided in different directions with others slotted in from inside or acquired from outside.

TOOL 7.25
SUCCESSION PLANNING

Strategic priorities:

Future capabilities required by those priorities:

Existing capabilities:

Gaps:

Current people to develop/plan to develop them:

People to recruit early on and develop/plan to develop them:

People to recruit later:

Copyright © PrimeGenesis® LLC. To customize this document, download Tool 7.25 from the First-Time Leader page on www.onboardingtools.com.

A Framework for Turning Individuals' Strengths into Team Synergies[17]

Employees perform at different levels, when on different teams, in different situations with different people. That probably makes sense to everyone. Why then do so few leaders spend so little time looking for synergies on their teams and so much time looking at individual performance? Because realizing synergies is hard work, and there has been no framework for doing so.

The Skills Plus Minus Framework

Phil and Allan Maymin and Eugene Shen began their "Skills Plus Minus" presentation at the MIT Sloan Sports Analytics Conference this year by asking who was basketball's better point guard from 2006 to 2008, Deron Williams, who then played for the Utah Jazz, or Chris Paul, who played for the New Orleans Hornets at the time.

The data is inconclusive with regard to the original question, but it does show that either player would have been even more valuable had he been on *the other team*. Had the Jazz and the Hornets done a one-for-one, straight-up trade, each team would have been better off. Their stars might or might not have performed better, but the entire teams would have performed better.

The presenters looked at individual skills and events including offensive and defensive ball handling, rebounding, and scoring. Then they looked at those skills and events in the company of other players to determine the positive and negative impact of players on each other. If two players each steal the ball from their opponents two times per game on their own, but together steal the ball five times per game when they are on the court together, that's a positive synergy.

Applying the Skills Plus Minus Framework to Your Team

Of course it's important to understand the strengths of the individuals on your team. That always will be important. But that's just the first step. The only way to optimize synergies on a team is to leverage differentiated individual strengths in complementary ways.

In a hypothetical example, one manager is particularly strong at managing details, one at operations, and one is particularly strong at encouraging creativity. Unfortunately, the guy with the operating strength is managing the group that needs to be creative; the more creative guy is managing a group that needed to pay attention to details; and the detail-oriented manager is trying to manage a complex operation. Moving each to the right role frees everyone up to perform better.

It's not just about the individuals. It's about the individuals in the context of the tasks that need to get done and the other individuals involved.

Let us propose five steps flowing from the BRAVE leadership model:

1. Understand the context in terms of where you choose to play and what matters.
2. Determine the attitude, relationships, and behaviors required to deliver what matters.
3. Evaluate each individual's attitudinal, relationship, and behavioral strengths.
4. Structure the work in a way that allows individuals to complement each other's strengths.
5. Monitor, evaluate, and adjust along the way.

The pivot point is leveraging complementary strengths across attitudinal, relationship, and behavioral elements. The specifics of those are going to be different in each different situation. That gets us back to the initial point. But now you've got a framework. So there's no excuse not to pay as much attention to potential team synergies as you do to individuals' strengths.

> Implications for you: Think team, not collection of individuals.

Transition (The *T* in ADEPT People Management)

There are some people moves that you must make quickly. On the other hand, generally you can evolve people into new roles over time.

Not all transitions are up. Some are across. Some are down. And some are out.

Across

Some people need to move to different roles at the same level to broaden their knowledge or skills or because their existing strengths can make a bigger impact somewhere else.

Down

Some people may want to move down to roles with less scope, responsibility, or stress as they move into different life stages: adding kids, spouse retiring, and so on.

Out

Some people are in the wrong role. They may never have been the right person for the role or the role may have changed around them. Either way, when it's time for them to go do something different, it's time.

The first time you have to move someone out or down is going to be painful—for them and for you. Remember that it's good that you're feeling pain. Deciding to move someone out of a role is a big decision not to be taken lightly. Remember also that the number one thing experienced leaders regret is not moving fast enough on people. And remember that the number one thing high performers want is for someone to get the low performers out of their way. So, think the moves through thoroughly. Then act decisively.

Leadership is about enabling and inspiring others to do their absolute best, together, to realize a meaningful and rewarding shared purpose. If everything stayed constant, people wouldn't have to transition to new roles. Everything is constantly changing, so transitioning people to new roles is often a big part of inspiring and enabling them to do their absolute best.

SUMMARY: HOW TO CONNECT

Everything you do or don't say, do, listen to, and observe communicates and drives how you connect—24/7, forever. Leverage a single, simplifying message in ongoing iterative conversations. Strive to make people feel proud through your words and actions.

- MAP your communication with your message, amplifiers, and perseverance.
- When onboarding yourself, get a head start, manage the message, build the team.
- Build an ADEPT team by acquiring, developing, encouraging, planning, and transitioning talent.

Chapter 8

BEHAVIORS: HOW YOU GET THINGS DONE THROUGH OTHER PEOPLE

Environment, values, attitude, and relationships all inform behaviors and what impact you and your team make. Ultimately, you lead with your feet, with what you do, more than with what you say. So focus everything and everyone on those few behaviors with the greatest impact.

Depending upon which part of the value chain you're focused on, different behaviors will have greater impacts.

- **Design**—If your focus is design, innovation is the key to your success. If you're not innovating, you're falling behind. And in a world of rapid change, that fall can happen very, very fast.
- **Build**—If your focus is building, supply chain negotiating has to be your bailiwick. You need to get clear on what core competencies you're going to keep in house to be best in the world and which you can outsource because being good enough is good enough.
- **Sell**—Everybody has to sell and market. As Drucker says, the purpose of business is to create customers. Pay attention to strategic selling and creative briefs here.
- **Distribute**—Distributing is like building, in that supply chain negotiating is key.
- **Support**—If your focus is support, make sure everyone in your organization is committed to the customer as boss and is prepared to react and respond as required by that boss.

DELEGATING, INNOVATING, AND NEGOTIATING

Learning to delegate is a nonoptional exercise. The core of leadership is inspiring and enabling others. This means giving them things to do that you could theoretically do yourself. The following piece from Forbes lays it out well.

Delegating[1]

Scope is a function of resources and time. If the scope of what you're trying to accomplish is too much to get done in a high-quality way in the time allotted, you have to add resources, add time, or cut back the scope. In other words, say no to some of the less important items and non-value-adding steps. Think in terms of your options for completing tasks:

1. Do well yourself
2. Do yourself, but just well enough
3. Delegate and supervise
4. Delegate and ignore
5. Do later
6. Do never

Working harder is often counterproductive. As Simpler Consulting CEO Marc Hafer explained to George, the world is full of heroes who get in the way—the "bright, passionate, compassionate ones who are blinded by their passion." They strive to "get it done" at any cost, not realizing the true cost is the diminished effort against other, higher value adding activities.

Gillian often works with a lot of new entrepreneurs who are working, literally, 24/7, hardly sleeping, barely eating, and having no social life whatsoever. This lifestyle is not only deconstructive; it's unhealthy and unsustainable. They are like hamsters in a wheel, always running but never getting anywhere. If you are in that position, you need to stop. Immediately. Figure out what you provide that is something no one else can and then do that. Outsource, delegate, hire for everything else. It's worth the money, because this is what will allow you to take the next step.

In Hafer's eyes, step one is figuring out which activities are actually valued by the end customer. You need to take into account stakeholders' concerns and requirements along the way, but if you're not defining true value in the end customer/patient/consumer's eyes, you're looking through the wrong lens.

With that in mind, more on your options:

Do Well Yourself

These are the things your end customer values most. You're going to say no and downplay, delegate, cut back, and avoid other things so you can spend more time on these critical activities. This is where you and your team need to strive for perfection. Doing well is an understatement. Here's where it's essential to do your absolute best.

Do Yourself, but Just Well Enough

You accept the need to do these things yourself. But they are not as important as some others. So, you should do them and do them well enough to satisfy the stakeholders who need them to fit into what they are doing for the end customer—and no better.

Delegate and Supervise

The items you delegate and supervise are important. You want them done well, but there isn't enough value in doing them yourself. Or perhaps, there are others who can do the work better than you. Either way, you care about these items enough to supervise the work.

Delegate and Ignore

Items you delegate and ignore are off your plate. You hope the people you delegate to will do them well, but they don't matter as much as other tasks. You're prepared to accept whatever results come to fruition.

Do Later

Things you decide to do later may get done eventually, but certainly not now. They are one step above the bottom rung and delaying them may cause stress with the people who need them now. That's a choice you've made in pursuit of the highest value-adding activities for the end customer.

Do Never

Not only do you think these tasks are bad ideas for you and for people you might delegate to, but you also believe they are just bad ideas. Here's your clearest "no." Not me. Not others. Not anyone. Not now. Not ever. Go away. (Harsh, but clear.)

The next time a task arises, ask yourself about the end value and then determine the best approach.

Implications for you: Figure out the very few things you must do yourself and delegate the rest.

Innovating

In general, you should delegate as much as you can to allow you to focus as much of your energy on your team and on innovating. If you don't understand the importance of team building, go back and reread Chapter 4. Regarding innovating, think about three phases:

1. Prepare in advance
2. Focus on solving problems
3. Follow through to turn ideas into reality and stay ahead of your competition

Preparing in Advance: MIT's Neri Oxman—the Beginner's Mind

Neri Oxman suggests the beginner's mind is filled with innocence. "As child you think you are shrinking when you see an airplane take off." Oxman and her Mediated Matters group at the MIT Media Lab have moved beyond "bio mimicry" to actually designing with nature in pursuit of bio-inspired fabrication. She told George about their new silk pavilion, actually created by 6,500 silkworms. She envisions scaling this idea with a swarm of 3-D printers to expand beyond any one printer's gantry as part of her search for "variations in kind," moving well beyond "better, faster, cheaper, bigger."

In an interview at the C2 Conference in Montreal, Oxman told George about her "fork in the road." She's a trained architect and designer. The choice she faced was whether to focus on design or go into research. She chose research because it gave her the opportunity to design her own technology. It allowed her to influence both products and processes—both influenced by nature.

She's a big proponent of variations in kind—true innovations. She's convinced these come from "being vulnerable," not so much from solving a problem as from innocence and different worldview. It's that different worldview that allows the innovator to come up with new to the world solutions when problems do come.

Focus on Solving Someone's Problem: Bobbi Brown

Bobbi Brown was on a TV shoot and had forgotten her eyeliner. To make do, she grabbed a Q-Tip and used it to brush some mascara on her eyelids, solving her immediate problem. The next morning she was surprised to see the mascara still in place. The gel in the mascara had made it last. She called her design team and had them mock up the first gel liner—now her most copied product. Many of Brown's innovations have come from thinking "It would make so much sense if . . ." She describes these as "random ideas mixed with common sense."

This was just one of the examples Brown shared with George. She also related how using a clean baby wipe to remove her makeup prompted her to create a baby-wipe-like makeup remover. And she told George about wanting to wear cowboy boots with jeans she had. When they wouldn't fit, she cut them off—the boots, not the jeans. These stories all go to her philosophy of having a clear vision, but then being open to change direction as needed. She's good at this because she seems to be able to understand what's needed next. Definitely a big idea to change direction before anyone else knows you need to.

George admits this was a difficult interview for him. He's still not sure he understands what the difference is between mascara and eyeliner. But Brown made it easy for George. She seemed to genuinely enjoy teaching a complete ignoramus (George) about what she did. George thinks that's part of what enables her to innovate and connect.

Follow-Through: Diane von Furstenberg

Diane von Furstenberg is clear that her wrap dress happened "by accident." Her original T-shirts morphed into wrap tops and then into wrap dresses. They caught on and have stayed in fashion for almost 40 years because they are "easy, proper, decent, and flattering and sexy." They may have happened by accident originally, but their ongoing success is directly related to von Furstenberg's drive to succeed on her own (at first), prove she was not a one-shot wonder (later), and leave a strong brand as her legacy (now).

TOOL 8.1
INNOVATION GUIDELINES

Innovation guidelines is an oxymoron in that the whole point of innovation is to do things in a new way. With that disclaimer, it's useful to think about preparing in advance, solving problems, and following through to turn ideas into reality.

1. Prepare in advance

2. Focus on solving problems

3. Follow through to turn ideas into reality and stay ahead of your competition

It's often difficult to separate the brand from the personality. On the one hand, while a major attribute of the Virgin brand is Richard Branson, and a major attribute of Apple was Steve Jobs, and a major attribute of Walmart was Sam Walton, in each of these cases the brand name and the personality are different. Those brands will survive their founders. It's harder when the founder's name and brand name match as they do with Diane von Furstenberg.

Of course there are examples of success. The Disney brand is thriving—perhaps because its sub-brands are anything but Mickey Mouse. McDonald's is a golden arch, and maybe a clown. Very, very few people think of Richard and Maurice.

Von Furstenberg has spent time thinking about the difference between the brand and herself. A big part of her follow-through is setting up the brand as her legacy: celebrating freedom, empowering women, color, print, bold, effortless, sexy, on the go. Of course she's a living example of the brand now. Over time, others need to step up as that example.

Negotiating

Negotiating is a part of leadership. Embrace it as a way to increase your leverage. You may find it helpful to follow our six-step negotiating process

1. Make a plan. (Identify the dimensions of the negotiations by answering these questions: What are my needs and concerns? What are the other party's needs and concerns?)
2. Get started. (Identify areas of agreement.)
3. Clarify positions. (State, support, and listen.)
4. Find alternatives.
5. Gain agreement. (Study proposals. Make concessions. Summarize. Test the agreements.)
6. Implement. (Communicate, deliver, and monitor.)

Make a Plan

There are two parts in making a plan: map out your needs and concerns, and map out their needs and concerns. Both should be done across all the critical dimensions of the negotiation. Your dimensions reflect your current criteria and long-term goals. It's important to know what you want and what you're willing to give up to get it. To complete this process, identify your walkaway, minimum, expected, and opening points for each critical dimension for you and for the other party.

For You *Walkaway* is the minimum you'll even begin to talk about. If the other party opens with something below that point, you walk away without even countering.

Minimum is the minimum acceptable.

Expected is where you think a deal will be done.

Opening is what you'd say first, if asked.

For Them *Walkaway* is the maximum they'll even begin to talk about. If you open with something above that point, they walk away without even countering.

Maximum is the maximum acceptable.

Expected is where they think a deal will be done.

Opening is what they'd say first, if asked.

In this example, on the dimension of base salary, there is a deal to be done. You, the new leader, are expecting a base salary of $225,000, but would take as low as $205,000. The company is expecting to pay you $210,000, but would pay as much as $230,000. Thus, there is a deal to be done somewhere between $205,000 and $230,000.

	You	Them	
		>250	Walkaway
Opening	240		
		230	Maximum
Expected	225		
		210	Expected
Minimum	205		
		200	Opening
Walkaway	<180		

Dimensions are important. The more dimensions you can negotiate on, the more room there is for give and take. For many people, a $200,000 straight salary is not as good as a $190,000 salary with a $10,000 per year travel allowance, or a salary of $190,000 and a bonus of up to $25,000. As the level of the role increases, the degrees of freedom on negotiations increase as well. A good way to learn what's possible is to use the Internet to research recent employment contracts for senior leaders of the company.

One executive got bored with his retirement. He applied for and was offered a job in a consulting group with compensation of a straight salary. His response was, "That's much less than I've been used to earning. But, given my stage in life, I could be happy with that annual salary if you gave me 20 weeks' vacation a year." They did.

We've used a base salary example because it's easy to illustrate. Use similar scales to map out all the important dimensions of whatever it is you're negotiating.

TOOL 8.2
NEGOTIATING

(For each dimension)
    My opening: _____
    My expected: _____
    My minimum: _____
    My walkaway: _____
    Their walkaway: _____
    Their maximum: _____
    Their expected: _____
    Their opening: _____
    Get Started.
    Somehow negotiations are always easier if you can start by agreeing.
Find the areas that you agree on and discuss those first.

Areas of Agreement

Areas for Debate

There's a framework for areas where there's a difference as well.

1. State your position.
2. Support your position with other information.
3. Listen to the other person's position and probe for understanding.
   Don't challenge at this point. Just seek to understand.

Find Alternatives

Look for ways to meet everyone's needs. Often this involves bringing
another dimension into the picture.

Gain Agreement

Again, there's a process for managing this:

1. Receive and make proposals
2. Receive and make concessions on different dimensions
3. Summarize the situation
4. Test agreements
5. Circle back to concessions until there's a complete agreement

Implement

Implementing is all about following through. You need to do what you say you're going to do. You need to communicate steps along the way. You need to deliver. You need to monitor all the parties so you know they are delivering as well.

SALES AND MARKETING

Selling and marketing are nonoptional exercises. You're going to need to offer things to your external and internal customers that they need and then you're going to need to convince them to buy what you're offering.

Purchase Funnel Tool and Discussion

Every purchase funnel there ever was, was and is a variation of AIDA: Awareness, Interest, Desire, Action. It's all about moving prospects through the funnel.

TOOL 8.3
PURCHASE FUNNEL

Every purchase funnel there ever was is a variation off AIDA: Awareness, Interest, Desire, Action. It's all about moving prospects through the funnel.

Awareness: Step 1 is making people aware of your offering.

Interest: Step 2 is sparking an initial interest in your offering.

Desire: Step 3 is creating a desire for your offering.

Action: Step 4 is closing the sale and moving the prospect to action.

Awareness: Step 1 is making people aware of your offering. This is the wide top of the funnel. The goal is to get people to notice you, to be aware of your offering.

Interest: Step 2 is sparking an initial interest in your offering. Once you've been noticed, you need to get people to take an interest. Think in terms of opting in, clicking through, or taking the meeting. Not even close to committing, but starting to move in the right direction.

Desire: Step 3 is creating a desire for your offering. This is the big step. This is about helping your prospects understand your offering, see how it solves their problem, and desire to move forward.

Action: Step 4 is closing the sale and moving the prospect to action. It's frightening how many sales go off the rails at this point. Cover your bases. Run through the tape. Close the sale.

Strategic Selling

Miller and Heiman are the masters of strategic selling. This is our quick summary of their years of experience.

Seven Steps

1. Set the single sales objective
   - Get all involved aligned around a clear, single, specific, measurable, time-bound, outcome-focused objective
2. Identify buying influences involved
   - ID economic, user, technical buyers and coaches (Economic buyers can say yes. User and technical buyers can say no.)
   - Understand their response modes: growth, trouble, even keel, overconfident
   - Understand the business results and personal wins they seek and red flags
3. Develop a sales strategy
   - Which resources to deploy against which buying influences at what time in what way
   - Think through components of conceptual selling
     - Understand/get > generate/give > select best/commit
     - Customer's concept
     - Sales call plan
4. Outline the proposition: Framework of offer
5. Presell the proposition: Testing and consulting
6. Propose the solution: Framework + customer's ideas and solution ideas
7. Close and follow up: Get to yes and then implement with all

TOOL 8.4
STRATEGIC SELLING

This is a cheat sheet for Miller and Heiman's strategic selling steps.

1. Set the single sales objective
   a. Specific, measurable, time-lined, outcome-focused
2. Identify the buying influences involved (economic, user, technical, coach)
   a. Response mode of each buyer (growth, trouble, even keel, over-confident), needs and wants
   b. Win results for each buyer
   c. Red flags
3. Develop a sales strategy
4. Outline the proposition
5. Presell the proposition
6. Propose the solution
7. Close and follow up

To customize this document, download Tool 8.4 from the First-Time Leader page on www.onboardingtools.com.

BRAVE Creative Briefs

Getting all the stakeholders aligned around a well-structured creative brief can save all sorts of disconnects, false starts, and rework on any creative project.

BRAVE creative briefs begin with a *project description/overview*. Think through and lay out the opportunity, approach, output, timing, and logistics as well as guidelines regarding decision making; resources, including people, budget, and operational tools; accountabilities, including milestones and timing; and consequences, including how to leverage the win.

It is particularly important to align expectations around five project questions (which by now should look a lot like the five core BRAVE questions):

1. Where to play?
2. What matters?
3. How to win?
4. How to connect?
5. What impact?

Environment—Where to Play?

First, describe the *context*. What we know about customers, collaborators, capabilities, competitors, and conditions (What?).

Then lay out *insights* drawn from the contextual data (So what?).

Values—What Matters?

Clarify the organization's overall *purpose* (Why?) and *objective* (What?) as well as how this project fits within that and helps move things in that direction.

Attitudes—How to Win?

Then lay out the strategy: broad choices (How?).

This should begin with the overall organizational or commercial strategy including the value proposition.

Lay out the positioning: target, frame of reference, benefit, support/attributes—permission to believe, brand character/attitude/voice.

Describe the business posture that goes hand in hand with strategy and adds richness to the strategy choices (e.g., proactive, fast follow, prepared, responsive).

Relationships—How to Connect?

This section lays out the mandatory elements focusing on the few critical elements that will drive the connection with the target audience. These could include components like visuals, selling idea, look, voice, communication points, information, as well as media and channels.

Behaviors—What Impact?

Finally, clarify the desired response: How the target will move through AIDA (Aware, Interest, Desire, Action) after experiencing the creative.

TOOL 8.5
BRAVE CREATIVE BRIEF

Project Description

Opportunity, approach, output, timing, logistics as well as guidelines regarding decision making; resources, including people, budget, and operational tools; accountabilities, including milestones and timing; and consequences including how to leverage the win.

It is particularly important to align expectations around five project questions, most likely starting with the last foundational question and working your way up the list:

1. Where to play?
2. What matters?
3. How to win?
4. How to connect?
5. What impact?

Environment—Where to Play?

Context: Customers, collaborators, capabilities, competitors, and conditions.
Insights drawn from the contextual data (So what?).

Values—What Matters?

Objective including the organization's overall purpose (Why?) and objective (What?) as well as how this project fits within that and helps move things in that direction.

Attitude—How to Win?

Strategy: Broad choices (How?).
Overall organizational or commercial strategy including value proposition.
Positioning: Target, frame of reference, benefit, support/attributes—permission to believe, brand character/attitude/voice.
Posture goes hand in hand with strategy and adds richness to the strategy choices.

Relationships—How to Connect?

Mandatory elements focused on the few critical elements that will drive the connection with the target audience. These could include components like visuals, selling idea, look, voice, communication points, information, as well as media and channels.

Behaviors—What Impact?

Desired response: How the target will move through AIDA (Aware, Interest, Desire, Action) after experiencing the creative.

Copyright © PrimeGenesis® LLC. To customize this document, download Tool 8.5 from the First-Time Leader page on www.onboardingtools.com.

OPERATING PROCESSES

Many of these are mechanical, but important.

Senior Management Trips

At some point you will get visited by senior management. They'll tell you it's an informal check-in and they don't want you to do any extra work to prepare. Don't believe them. Don't get us wrong. They mean what they say. But they will be comparing the greeting you and your team give them to the greeting they get from other groups who have done all sorts of extra work to prepare. Do the extra work. Be prepared.

We suggest the following as key areas for attention.

Objectives: Get clear on senior management's objectives for the trip—and your objectives. Think through what you want senior management to know, do, and feel, and how you can leverage their presence to move your priorities forward.

Itinerary: Make sure everyone is clear on all the logistics around arrivals, departures, meetings, locations, people, dress—in excruciating detail.

Key peoples' responsibilities: Get clear on who is going to do what, when, with what resources in line with your objectives and itinerary.

Remarks/bullet points: Target/key message points. This is particularly important if you're going to ask senior management to talk to customers, employees, allies, regulators, or the press. Take charge of briefing them. (And, of course, do the same with anyone who's going to be meeting with or presenting to senior management.)

Gifts: Be clear and prepared for who is going to give what to whom—and what cannot be given in light of your own cultural, regulatory, or ethical concerns. (Just to be clear, there are no restrictions of any sort on any of you sending Gillian or George random amounts of money at any time as a way to say thank you for this wonderful book.)

Briefing book: Prepare a briefing document with a market review, background on allies, customers, politicians, specific circumstances, and so on. Everything communicates. Spend time on the content, not money on the presentation.

Event handling: Have appropriate handlers/interpreters around to help deal with logistics and cultural nuances. Remember there are cultural differences between organizations as well as regions.

Plan to debrief: Probably two debriefs—one with senior management and one for your team.

Follow-ups: As part of the debrief, clarify who is sending whom follow-up letters, gifts, pictures, and so on.

TOOL 8.6
SENIOR MANAGEMENT TRIP PLANNING

Objectives:

Itinerary: Arrivals, departures, meetings, locations, people, dress

Key people's responsibilities:

Remarks/bullet points—target/key message points:

Gifts:

Briefing book: Market review, background on allies, customers, politicians, specific circumstances

Event handling: Handler/interpreter—logistics, cultural nuances

Plan to debrief:

Follow-ups: Letters, gifts, pictures, and so on

Copyright © PrimeGenesis® LLC. To customize this document, download Tool 8.6 from the First-Time Leader page on www.onboardingtools.com.

Milestone Management

Let's make sure we're all dealing with the same definitions:

Objectives: Broadly defined, qualitative performance requirements.
Goals: The quantitative measures of the objectives that define success.

Strategies: Broad choices around how the team will achieve its objectives.

To those add:

Milestones: Checkpoints along the way to achieving objectives and goals.

NASA and the Apollo 13 ground team provide a useful example of this. The objective of getting the astronauts back home alive after the explosion in space was compelling, but overwhelming.

It was easier to work through milestones one by one:

1. Turn the ship around so it would get back to earth.
2. Manage the remaining power so it would last until they were back.
3. Fix the carbon monoxide problem so the air remained breathable.
4. Manage reentry into the atmosphere so the ship didn't burn up.

The power of milestones is that they let you know how you're doing along the way and give you the opportunity to make adjustments. They also give you the comfort to let your team run toward the goal without your involvement, as long as the milestones are being reached as planned.

You might evaluate your team's journey to a goal like this:

Worst case	The team misses a goal and doesn't know why.
Bad	The team misses a goal and knows why.
Okay	The team misses a milestone but adjusts to make the overall goal.
Good	The team anticipates risk as it goes along to make key milestones.
Best	The team hits all milestones on the way to goal . . . (in your dreams).

Imagine that you set a goal of getting from London to Paris in five-and-a-half hours. Now imagine that you choose to drive.

You set off on your journey.

It takes you 45 minutes to get from central London to the outskirts of London.

Thirty minutes after that, you wonder, "How's the trip going so far?"

You have no clue.

You might be on track. You might be behind schedule. But it's early in the trip so you probably think that you can make up time later if you need to. So you're not worried.

If, on the other hand, you had set the following milestones, you would be thinking differently:

- Central London to outskirts of London: 30 minutes.
- Outskirts of London to Folkestone: 70 minutes.
- Channel Crossing: load—20 minutes; cross—20 minutes; unload—20 minutes.
- Calais to Paris: three hours.

If you had set a milestone of getting to the outskirts of London in 30 minutes and it took you 45 minutes, you would know you were behind schedule. Knowing that you were behind schedule, you could then take action on alternative options. The milestone would make you immediately aware of the need to adjust to still reach your overall goal.

You and your team are going to miss milestones. It is not necessary to hit all your milestones. What is essential is that you and your team have put in place a mechanism to identify reasonable milestones so that you have checkpoints that allow you to anticipate and adjust along the way.

Manage Milestone Updates with a Three-Step Process

Deploying a mutually supportive team-based follow-up system helps everyone improve performance versus goals. Organizations that have deployed this process in their team meetings have seen dramatic improvements in team performance. Follow these three steps as well as the prep and post instructions laid out here and in Tool 8.7 and you'll be well on your way to ensuring that the team achieves their desired results on time.

Prep   Circulate individual milestone updates to the team to read before each meeting so you can take update sharing and reporting off the agenda, while still deploying a disciplined process to make sure that information flows where it needs to go. Leaders often skip this step much to the team's detriment. It seems like an easy process to put in place, but we've heard every reason in the book as to why it has not been implemented.

Usually there are some logistic protocols that need to be established, tracking method choices, and time frames established for submitting and distribution of information before the process can begin. Make these choices as soon as practical. You must require that everyone complete the update and pre-meeting review on time. If you allow excuses here, the rest of the process takes a hit.

Yes, it can be a pain to get it started, but once it is embedded as a team expectation, you'll be thankful that you endured the brief period of pain.

Step 1   Use the first half of each meeting for each team member to headline wins, learning, and areas in which the person needs help from other team members, but do not work through items at this point. Discussing items here reinforces a first-come, first-served mentality where the people who share later in the order tend to get squeezed for time. The "help from other team members" is often the most important part of the meeting. Each of these items should be captured. It's a good idea to keep a set time limit for each individual update. Those who tend to be long-winded might not like it, but the rest of the participants will appreciate it. A tight and controlled limit goes a long way to making the meetings more dynamic.

Step 2   Pause at the meeting's halfway point to prioritize items for discussion so the team can discuss items in the right priority instead of first come, first served. These won't necessarily be the universally most important items because some items should be worked with a different group or subset of the team. You should make note of those items in the meeting, but defer them to another meeting where the full and proper group can address them. Instead, give priority to the most important items for this team to work on as a team, at this time. Tend to give priority to items that are off target or in danger, or to areas where help is needed. Develop a list in descending order of priority.

Step 3   Use the second part of the meeting to discuss, in order, the priority list you determined to be the overall team's most important issues and opportunities. The expectation is that the team won't get through all the items. That's okay because you're working the most important items first (which is why you paused to prioritize items). This is the time to figure out how to adjust as a team to make the most important goals, all the while reinforcing predetermined decision rights.

Post   Defer other items to the next meeting or to a separate meeting. Update the tracking reports with any changes or new directions. Communicate major shifts to those key stakeholders who need to know.

BRAVE TIP 1

Anticipation is the key: at first, milestones will go from "on track" to "oops we missed" with no steps in between. You'll know the process is working well when people are surfacing areas they might miss if they don't get help from others. Focus your love and attention on these might-miss items to get the team to help. It will make people feel good about surfacing issues and will encourage them to bring future issues to the group for help.

BRAVE TIP 2

Banish the first-come, first-served mentality. This milestone process is easy to deploy for disciplined people and teams. It is hard for less disciplined people because they want to work items first come, first served. Resist that. Follow the process. You'll learn to love it. (Well, maybe not love it, but you will appreciate it. It will strengthen your team.)

BRAVE TIP 3

Integrate across instead of managing down: the milestone meetings are great forums for making connections across groups. The further you rise in the organization, the more time you'll spend integrating across and the less time you'll spend managing down. Most don't like to be tightly managed or have their decision rights compromised, but everyone appreciates improved information flows and linking projects and priorities across groups.

TOOL 8.7
MILESTONE MANAGEMENT

Milestone Management Process

Leader conducts a weekly or biweekly milestones management meeting with his or her team.

Prior to Milestones Management Meetings

Each team member submits his or her updates.
Designated person compiles and circulates updated milestones in advance of the meeting.

At Milestones Management Meetings

First part of the meeting:
Each team member gives a five-minute update in the following format: most important wins, most important learnings, areas where he or she needs help.

(continued)

Midpoint of the meeting:
    The leader orders topics for discussion in order of priority.
Second part of the meeting:
    Group discusses priority topics in order, spending as much time as
    necessary on each topic.

The remaining topics are deferred to the next milestones management meeting or a separate meeting. Key items are updated and communicated.

Milestones Tracking

Milestones Priority Programs	When	Who	Status	Discussion/Help Needed
			on-track	
			lagging, but will be made up	
			heading for a miss	

Copyright © PrimeGenesis® LLC. To customize this document, download Tool 8.7 from the First-Time Leader page on www.onboardingtools.com.

Royal Caribbean's CEO Exemplifies How to Leverage Milestones[2]

Tracking milestones is not a revolutionary business idea. However, the idea of using them as a team-building tool is new to most leaders and their teams. Royal Caribbean's CEO, Richard Fain, fully appreciates the power of milestones and exemplifies how other leaders can utilize them to keep projects on track and recognize employee achievements.

Milestones for Project Management   Fain's emphasis on milestones is not a surprise, as ship builders have been leveraging milestones' emotional impact for millennia. Ship builders celebrate keel laying as the formal start of construction, naming, stepping the mast (accompanied by placing coins under the mast for good luck), christening (accompanied by breaking a bottle of champagne over the bow), a whole range of trials, sail away, hand over, and my personal favorite—onboarding the new captain.

As Fain explained to me,

> If you don't establish early on key milestones—long-term milestones rather than the short-term milestones—you get caught in the "next week" syndrome. I can't think of a project that we are doing or have done (during which we do not) get to a key point and everybody says "We're going to know so much more next week or the week after." And so the focus shifts to next week or the week after and we all desperately wait for that period. Meanwhile the longer-term milestone goes by the wayside.
>
> So what we tend to do is say we need to know where we're going. We need to know what we expect to have at the end. And so we talk a lot about our end point rather than the waypoints.

Milestones for Team Building   What Fain does particularly well is leverage milestones both as a way to keep big projects on track—like building a ship, a new computer system, or a major marketing program—and to keep smaller projects on track. They also provide him with excuses to encourage all involved along the way. He goes to major events. He participates in new ship trials so he can experience the excitement of how the ship performs. Then he shares that excitement with others in his meetings, talks, videos, blog, and all forms of communication.

In an interview with Knowledge@Wharton, Fain talked about "letting people know you care is of surpassing value." The links with his approach to milestones come through. He's built a team of people that try to surpass—and he gives them milestones to beat. He knows that people value recognition—and he leverages milestone ceremonies to recognize their achievements whether it's the first time people can actually walk on board and see a ship, or the first look at the prototype of a new computer system.

Royal Caribbean likes to build models so people can see and touch tangible things and know what they are going to do. They model staterooms, software, and marketing materials. When a project gets to a certain point, they give it a name. "It's interesting how giving that project a name galvanizes people around it—because it makes it more tangible to them."

One of its big projects was the creation of a central gathering area on the ship *Oasis of the Seas*. This area—which is aptly named Central Park—is located in the middle of the ship and opens to the sky for five decks. To celebrate the design, Royal Caribbean created a full-size model of part of this open space in the massive hangar-like building where parts of the ship were being built in Finland. Also, the company treated the whole team to an alfresco fine dining experience so they could celebrate the space.

It was a magical evening. . . . We were having a lovely cruise dinner in Finland (in early Spring—when it's still cold outside). . . . It made us all realize how special the space would be and that it was worthy of the effort to really make sure that not only was the overall space good, but that all the details were perfect.

Once they know you care, then you can challenge them. As Fain said in a recent interview with Adam Bryant for the *New York Times*, "My experience is that people love to be challenged. If the challenge is reasonable, or even slightly unreasonable, they love it and they rise to the occasion. There's just no question. People love to be challenged and they love to show off their skills and talents." Aggressive, but doable milestones create just such a challenge.

Establish a Process to Track Milestones   Compiling milestones is a waste of time if you do not have an efficient, effective, and clear process in place to track them—and avoid the "next week" syndrome.

Define them and begin tracking and managing them immediately. Use the process to establish and reinforce expected team norms.

1. Get milestones in place.
2. Track them and manage them as a team on a frequent and regular basis.
3. Implement a milestone management process with a particular emphasis on solving problems and celebrating wins—as a team (with your own version of a lovely al fresco cruise dinner in a warehouse).

Quarterly Cadence Framework

Following are important elements to consider on a regular basis.

People

Succession Planning   Align the longer term organizational development plans with the longer term (three-plus years) strategic plan. Do this on an annual basis.

Performance Management and Talent Review   Track progress of the longer term succession plan and the corresponding talent needs (one-year horizon). Do this on an annual basis.

Plans

Strategic Review, Refresh, and Plan   Conduct a detailed long-term look at the business (three-year horizon), leading to choices around how to create and allocate resources over that longer-term horizon. Do this on an annual basis.

Operational Review, Refresh, and Plan   Ensure that the right operational plans (one-year horizon) are in place that will enable you to deliver the next year's goals. Do this on an annual basis.

Practices

Business Reviews and Plan Updates   Track progress in the context of the operational plan (one-year horizon) and make midcourse adjustments along the way. Do this quarterly.

Milestone Updates and Adjustment   Track the monthly milestones to keep the team focused on the most important thing, as a team. Do this monthly, unless particular milestones are falling off target, in which case you should increase the frequency until the milestones are back on track.

Thinking about these things with these horizons allows you to have a good balance between long-term thinking and short-term execution. A number of our clients have blended these into an annual/quarterly/monthly meeting schedule. The idea is to have a meeting every month with time added once each quarter to deal with longer term issues. It is a cycle with each piece feeding into the next. Use this cadence as a starting point and then adjust it to meet your organizational needs without dropping any key pieces.

Cadence   Monthly milestone updates with quarterly meetings to work business reviews/plan updates each quarter and one of these:

Q1—Talent Review
Q2—Strategic Plan
Q3—Succession Plan
Q4—Operational Plan

TOOL 8.8
QUARTERLY CADENCE

Q1	Talent Review Business Review and adjustment

(continued)

Q2	Strategic Plan Business Review and adjustment
Q3	Succession Plan Business Review and adjustment
Q4	Operating Plan Business Review and adjustment

BRAVE CRISIS MANAGEMENT

The New Leader's 100-Day Action Plan lays out a sequential methodology for leaders and their teams to get done in 100 days what normally takes 6 to 12 months. In a crisis or disaster, this time frame is woefully inadequate as teams need a way to get done in 100 hours what normally takes weeks or months. This requires an iterative instead of sequential approach. That methodology follows.[3]

Start with the basic premise that leadership is about inspiring and enabling others. Enhance that with Leonard Lodish's idea that "it is better to be vaguely right than precisely wrong."[4] Then add Darwin's point that "it is not the strongest of the species that survives, nor the most intelligent, but the one most responsive to change."[5] Add it all up and you get leading through a crisis being about inspiring and enabling others to get things vaguely right quickly, and then adapt along the way—with clarity around direction, leadership, and roles.

This plays out in three steps of a disciplined iteration in line with the overall purpose:

1. *Prepare in advance.* The better you have anticipated possible scenarios, the more prepared you are, the more confidence you will have when crises strike.

2. *React to events.* The reason you prepared is so that you all can react quickly and flexibly to the situation you face. Don't overthink this. Do what you prepared to do.
3. *Bridge the gaps.* In a crisis, there is inevitably a gap between the desired and current state of affairs. Rectify that by bridging those gaps in the
   - **Situation:** Implementing a response to the current crisis
   - **Response:** Improving capabilities to respond to future crises
   - **Prevention:** Reducing the risk of future crises happening in the first place

Along the way, keep the ultimate purpose in mind. It needs to inform and frame everything you do over the short, mid, and long term as you lead *through* a crisis instead of merely *out* of a crisis. Crises change your organization. Be sure that the choices you make during crises change you in ways that move you toward your purpose and not away from your core vision and values.

Prepare in Advance

One life squad ran a drill in conjunction with the fire and police departments. It involved a car running off the road and down an embankment. The squad had to get down the embankment, treat urgent trauma, and package the victims for the fire department to lift out of the ditch and load into ambulances. Twenty minutes into the drill was this exchange:

> "Where's my baby?"
> "Your daughters are in the other ambulance."
> "But where's my baby?"

It turned out that in addition to the four adults and teenagers, there was another victim. Lesson learned: make sure you account for all victims.

Preparing in advance is about building general capabilities and capacity—not specific situational knowledge. For the most part, there is a finite set of the most likely, most devastating types of crises and disasters that are worth preparing for. Think them through. Run the drills. Capture the general lessons so people can apply them flexibly to the specific situations they encounter.[6] Have resources ready to be deployed when those disasters strike.

React to Events

Our fight or flight instincts evolved to equip us for moments like this. If the team has the capabilities and capacity in place, turn them loose to respond to the events. This is where all the hard work of preparation pays off.

Bridge the Gaps

Although first responders should react in line with their training, keep in mind that random, instinctual, uncoordinated actions by multiple groups exacerbate chaos. Stopping everything until excruciatingly detailed situation assessments have been fed into excruciatingly detailed plans that get approved by excruciatingly excessive layers of management leads to things happening too late. The preferred methodology for what Harrald calls the integration phase is to pause to accelerate, get thinking and plans vaguely right quickly, and then get going to bridge the gaps.[7]

Apply the BRAVE framework here on an accelerated basis, working through the five questions: where to play, what matters, how to win, how to connect, and what impact.

Where to Play—Situational Questions

Keep in mind the physical, political, and emotional context.

- What do we know, and not know, about what happened and its impact (facts)?
- What are the implications of what we know and don't know (conclusions)?
- What do we predict may happen (scenarios)?
- What resources and capabilities do we have at our disposal (assets)? Gaps?
- What aspects of the situation can we turn to our advantage?

What Matters—Objectives and Intent

Armed with answers to those questions, think through and choose the situational objectives and intent. What are the desired outcomes of leading through the crisis? What is the desired end state? This is a critical component of direction and a big deal.

For example, when a glass water bottle capper at a major beverage company went bad, grinding screw top threads into glass chips, the objective and intent were (1) stop the damage and (2) protect the brand.

How to Win—Priorities

The American Red Cross provides relief to victims of disasters. In doing that, the prioritization of shelter, food, water, medicine, and emotional support varies by the type of disaster. If a fire destroys someone's home in the winter, shelter takes precedence. On the other hand, if a reservoir gets contaminated, the critical priority is getting people clean water.

In general, priority order should be physical, reputational, financial. If you have to sacrifice your reputation to save lives, so be it. If lives are not at stake, but you have to pay a financial penalty to protect your reputation, that's the right choice. Think physical risk, reputational risk, financial risk—in that order.

These examples illustrate the importance of thinking through the priorities for each individual situation—and each stage of a developing crisis. The choices for isolating, containing, controlling, and stabilizing the immediate situation likely will be different from the priorities for the midterm response, getting resources in the right place, and then delivering the required support over time. Those will be different from the priorities involved in repairing the damage from the crisis or disaster and preventing its reoccurrence.

Get the answer to the question Where do we focus our efforts first? and the priority choices are clear.

How to Connect—Communication

Get priorities communicated to all, perhaps starting with a set of meetings to

- Recap current situation and needs, and what has already been accomplished.
- Agree on objectives, intent, priorities, and phasing of priorities.
- Agree on action plans, milestones, role sort, communication points, plans, and protocols.

These are the basic building blocks of most leadership communication plans. However, a crisis is better managed by using an iterative approach than by using the more normal sequential approach. This is why we recommend early meetings to jump-start strategic, operational, and organizational processes all at the same time, getting things vaguely right quickly and then adapting to new information along the way.

What Impact—Bridge the Gap between the Desired and Current State

Follow these steps in bridging the gaps between the desired and current state:

Support team members in implementing plans while gathering more information concurrently.

Complete situation assessment and midterm prioritization and plans.

Conduct milestone update sessions daily or more frequently as appropriate:
- Update progress on action plans with focus on wins, learning, areas needing help.
- Update situation assessment.
- Adjust plans iteratively, reinforcing the expectation of continuous adjustment.

Overcommunicate at every step of the way to all the main constituencies. Your message and main communication points will evolve as the situation and your information about the situation evolve. This makes the need that much greater for frequent communication updates within the organization, with partner organizations, and with the public. Funneling as much as possible through one spokesperson will reduce misinformation. Do not underestimate the importance of this.

First officer Jeff Skiles was flying the airplane that took off, ran into a flock of birds, and lost both its engines. At that point, Captain Chesley Sullenberger chose to take over. With his "My aircraft" command, followed by Skiles's "Your aircraft" response, control was passed to "Sully," who safely landed the plane on the Hudson River. Only one pilot can be actually flying a plane at one time. Two people trying to land the same plane at the same time simply does not work.

The same is true for crisis and disaster management. Only one person can be flying any effort or component at a time. A critical part of implementation is clarifying and reclarifying who is doing what and who is making what decisions at what point—especially as changing conditions dictate changes in roles and decision-making authority within and across organizations. Make sure the hand-offs are as clean as the one on Sully and Skiles's flight.

Bridge the gaps between desired and current response and desired and most recent crisis prevention (improving things and reducing risks for the future).

At the end of the crisis, conduct an after-action review looking at

- What actually happened? How did that compare with what we expected to happen?
- What impact did we have? How did that compare with our objectives?
- What did we do particularly effectively that we should do again?
- What can we do even better the next time in terms of risk mitigation and response?

Crisis Management Summary

Leading through a crisis is about inspiring and enabling others to get things vaguely right quickly and adapt iteratively along the way—with clear direction, leadership, and roles.

Follow these three steps:

1. **Prepare in advance.** Preparation breeds confidence. Think through your own crisis management protocols. Pre-position resources. ID and train crisis management teams.
2. **React to events.** Leverage that preparation to respond quickly and flexibly in the moment. This requires courage on the part of management to let people do what they are prepared to do without much over-supervision early on. However, it is important to instill an "ask for help early," rather than a "wait until we are overwhelmed," attitude in the responders.[8]
3. **Bridge the gaps.** Do this between desired and current situations, response capabilities, and prevention, supporting team members in implementing purpose-driven, priority-focused plans while gathering more information concurrently.

TOOL 8.9
CRISIS MANAGEMENT 100-HOUR
ACTION PLAN

Organization's Purpose

Update

 Wins—Share and celebrate the good things that have already happened

 Learning—Share learning that can help others

 Help—Highlight areas needing more support

Physical, Political, Emotional, Reputational, Financial Context

 What do we know, and not know about what happened and its impact (facts)?

 What are the implications of what we know and don't know (conclusions)?

 What do we predict may happen (scenarios)?

 What resources and capabilities do we have at our disposal (assets)? Gaps?

 What aspects of the situation can we turn to our advantage?

(continued)

Situational Objectives and Intent

Priority 1: _____Leader: _____

Actions: _____When: _____Who: _____

Actions: _____When: _____Who: _____

Actions: _____When: _____Who: _____

Priority 2: _____Leader: _____

Actions: _____When: _____Who: _____

Actions: _____When: _____Who: _____

Actions: _____When: _____Who: _____

Priority 3: _____Leader: _____

Actions: _____When: _____Who: _____

Actions: _____When: _____Who: _____

Actions: _____When: _____Who: _____

Communication

Primary Spokesperson: _____
Backup: _____
Message: _____
Communication Points:

1. _____

2. _____

3. _____

Protocols

Next Team Call/Meeting: _____
Exception Guidelines:

Planning Your Future When the Future You Had Planned Goes Awry—Rick Eno, Metabolix[9]

When the future you had planned goes awry, hit restart, adjust, and realign your people, plans, and practices around your shared purpose.

Ever since the movie *The Graduate* in 1967, it's popular knowledge that "there's a great future in plastics." Biodegradable plastics innovator Metabolix certainly recognizes this fact. And its joint venture partner ADM believed it too—until it didn't.

On the afternoon of January 9, 2012, Metabolix received a fax from ADM terminating their eight-year relationship. As part of the joint venture, ADM had invested about $300 million into a plant to manufacture Metabolix's plastics in return for half the joint venture's profits.

As Metabolix CEO Rick Eno told me, larger companies have "optionality" and flexibility. ADM chose to redeploy its resources elsewhere. Unfortunately, Metabolix had gone public in 2006 partially based on the expected earnings stream from its joint venture with ADM. For them, the news was "pretty shocking" and they "did not have options in development. [They] had to start at square one."

Shared Purpose

Where did Metabolix begin? First, it reconfirmed its shared purpose: delivering sustainable solutions to the plastics, chemicals, and energy industries. That part was easy. The world needs these solutions. The market is growing 20 percent annually. With hundreds of patents and customers who offered to help, Metabolix chose to keep going.

Plans

The hard part was figuring out *how* to keep going. As leaders of a public company, Eno and his team needed to convince themselves (and their stakeholders) of the value of their mission and the capabilities to get it done. Eno told George this involved "a lot of work, soul searching, and analysis."

In the absence of a deep-pocketed partner, Metabolix changed its approach from pursuing large volumes over time to going after "valuable niches." A Spanish supplier replaced ADM's 50,000-ton joint venture plant with a 10,000-ton toll manufacturing deal. With that in place, Eno and his team shifted focus to a more select group of customers from which they could earn higher margins: value, not volume.

People

The shift from joint venture partner to toll manufacturer created the need for Metabolix to put in place several new capabilities. It needed to be able to manage

- Manufacturing
- Supply chain
- Europe (as they had relied on ADM's presence there)

The good news was that Metabolix was filled with "extremely motivated people." They were "going to take that hill" and volunteered to make whatever adjustments were necessary.

Practices

Eno took George through the practices that needed to change given the company's new reality. They

- Accelerated the pace of decision making—not hard since they were on their own instead of part of a joint venture.
- Implemented task/project-focused teams.
- Created robust and very short-term target setting, especially around manufacturing and customers.

It's still early days and not yet clear how successful Metabolix will be in the long run. But, they were able to adjust enough so there will be a long run.

SUMMARY: WHAT IMPACT

Environment, values, attitude, and relationships all inform behaviors and what impact you and your team make.

- Lead with your feet, with what you do, more than with what you say.
- Focus everything and everyone on those few behaviors with the greatest impact.
- Focus the team on what creates the most value for your team's customers across the value chain: design–build–sell–deliver–support.

Part III

LEADING SMALL, MEDIUM, AND LARGE TEAMS

Chapter 9

WITH TEAMS OF LESS THAN 10 PEOPLE, ADOPT A START-UP MIND-SET

WHY THE WAY YOU LEAD TODAY IS GOING TO BE INADEQUATE TOMORROW[1]

Just when you think you've got your team and situation figured out, things change—especially when you're growing. Leading teams of less than 10 people is different from leading teams of 10 to 30 is different again from leading teams of more than 30.

With Teams of Less Than 10 People, Adopt a Start-Up Mind-Set

If you are starting or joining a small team, lead with environment and values. The critical questions are where to play and what matters. Build everything else on these over time. Play where you can solve someone's problem. Then assemble your early team of complementary partners. Not everyone on the team needs to have strategic, operational, and organizational strengths. But someone on the team should, and all must buy into the same values.

Devanshi Garg was a part of the founding team that led the introduction of Icreon Tech to the United States. In the team's early days Garg acted like "we were building our founding team" even though it was part of a larger company. Her early days' mantra was that the "first few people must fit the Icreon DNA— but with unique personality" and an ability to solve clients' problems while being "flexible, adaptable, wearing multiple hats."

- Start by focusing on problem solving, values, and creating momentum.

Lead Teams of 10 to 20 Like an Extended Family

Once the team grows beyond a nuclear family with everyone reporting to one leader, the nature of how the team works changes. At this point, attitude starts to become more important. Get the strategy set, deciding at what you are going to be best in the world, and use that as your guide for how to grow the team and which capabilities to add first. With teams of 10 to 30 people or so, you'll know everyone and can treat them like extended family. Even so, this is the time to implement rudimentary people-management and operating practices.

As the Icreon U.S. team grew to this size she found that her internal communication needed to be "more strategic." Early on, with a small team in a small space with no privacy, communication happened whether people wanted it to or not. As the team grew she had to create events, check-ins, and opportunities for team members to do things together—like running a New York Marathon as Team Icreon or going to a Broadway play together.

- As the team grows, emphasize differentiation and culture.

If You're Leading More Than 30 People, Hierarchy Is Your Friend

If the team has more than 30 people, you need to get over your natural abhorrence of hierarchy and start substituting some organizational and operating processes for your ability to know everyone on the team. With this size team, lead with relating and behaviors (how to connect, what impact). Work on the organization. Put in place enabling practices to scale. And remember the number one job of the leader is to own and reinforce vision and values. This gets ever more important (and complicated) as the organization grows.

Garg knows that as the team continues to grow, she'll need to embrace more hierarchy. However, she hopes she can build a "cellular organization" where the different cells exchange ideas as easily as strangers exchange recipes.

- Work on the organization and enabling practices while reinforcing vision and values.

This and the next two chapters deal with these three different-sized teams. Let's start with your start-up team here.

If you are starting up a team or joining a small start-up team, lead with environment and values. The critical questions for teams of this size are where to play and what matters. You'll build everything else on these over time. Play where you can solve someone's problem. Then assemble your early team of complementary partners. Not everyone on the team needs to have strategic, operational, and organizational strengths. But someone on the team should, and all must buy into the same values.

In the beginning there is an idea. There's a problem to be solved. Someone decides to solve it and begins to put together a team to do so. This is where starter teams come in. The nature of these teams is that you, as leader, know everyone on the team. Sometimes you're the one with the idea and you're the one creating the team from scratch. Sometimes it's someone else's idea and they've asked you to build the team. Sometimes the team is in place and you take it over. In all cases, focus on the problem and its solution.

In this chapter we'll apply the frameworks and tools from previous chapters to help you lead a start-up team, think through where to play and what matters, and set the stage for future growth. Let's begin with where to play.

SOLVE A PROBLEM SHARED BY MANY[2]

People get jobs by solving someone's problem. People build businesses with systemic ways to solve a problem shared by many others. Just knowing about a problem is not enough. You have to fix it. If you can build a repeatable way to fix it, then you can build a business.

Ted Schenberg and his business partner Travis Morgan initially invested in Strand Analytical Laboratories as a "small, underperforming company," as they told George in a recent interview. It had "great technical capabilities, but had no adult supervision." Its forensic DNA lab did great work for the law enforcement community, but was not able to move samples through the lab fast enough to make any money.

Job one was fixing the lab through process engineering. (How they did that is a different story. For our purposes here it is enough to know that they did it well enough to become cash flow positive—giving them the opportunity to leverage their technical strengths in new ways.)

Although Schenberg admits he "couldn't even spell DNA," he could watch television. He was struck by an October 2007 feature on NBC's *Today Show* talking about how "because of a mislabeled tissue sample that led to a misdiagnosis, Darrie Eason had both of her breasts removed to save her from a cancer that she never had." Schenberg and his partners realized that Strand's forensic DNA matching technology could prevent this sort of mistake.

Schenberg walked George through the five-step process he and his partners used to get from that moment to a business expansion:

1. **Confirm your hypothesis:** Schenberg called his colleague Dr. Peter Knapp, who confirmed anecdotally that this type of mix-up occurs on a periodic basis. (Since then, a Washington University study has shown that

there is a 1.9 percent incidence of undetected switching or contamination errors among patients' biopsy samples.)

2. **Solve the problem:** By utilizing Strand's forensic DNA matching capabilities and rapid turnaround of results, patients undergoing a biopsy for suspected cancer could be sure that their biopsy results are in fact theirs prior to any treatment. Here Schenberg and his partners got Strand's technical people engaged. This was relatively easy since the idea of helping patients played to the same core values as provided by their forensic DNA work: doing public good—keeping bad guys (or bad cells) off the street and protecting good guys (or good cells).

3. **Prototype:** This is the difference between a project and a business. Solving the problem once is interesting. Solving it on a repeatable basis is marketable. It's also essential for getting licensed (to perform highly complex medical testing), which Strand started pursuing at this point along with developing a sample collection system with help from Dr. Knapp.

4. **Test:** The team conducted alpha tests to get the bugs out and then beta tests to prove their concept in the field.

5. **Commercialize:** The important thing to remember here is that the strengths required to develop and test prototypes are not the same as the strengths required to commercialize them. Schenberg and his partners appointed lab industry veteran Ken Cerney as president. He "knew how to take our test to market," branding their solution as the know error® system and helping to build the business.

Implications for you:

1. As a prelude, find an unsolved problem shared by many people.
2. Build the strengths required to solve that problem. Solve the problem. Systematize the solutions to maximize the impact.
3. Follow through to market that solution broadly.

Net, play where you can solve someone's problem. Your purpose will flow from that. Be flexible.

ASSEMBLE A TEAM OF LIKE-MINDED INDIVIDUALS WITH DIVERSE STRENGTHS

There's not a lot of margin for error on a small team. Everyone needs to contribute to the purpose. You need people that get along with each other and share a commitment to solving the problem you're focused on. But you need diversity.

Lessons from "The Animal School" Fable in Leveraging Strengths[3]

The following is an adaptation of George Reavis's fable "The Animal School," originally written in 1940, when he was superintendent of the Cincinnati Public Schools:

> The animals organized a school to help their children deal with the problems of the new world. And to make it easier to administer the curriculum of running, climbing, swimming, and flying, they decided that all their children would take all the subjects. This produced some interesting issues.
>
> The duck was excellent in swimming but relatively poor in running, so he devoted himself to improving his running through extra practice. Eventually, his webbed feet got so badly worn that he dropped to only average in swimming. But average was acceptable in this school so nobody worried about that, except the duck.
>
> The rabbit had a nervous breakdown because the other animals said she looked like a rat when she jumped in the water for swimming class and all her hair got matted down.
>
> In the climbing class, the eagle beat all the others to the top of the tree, but kept insisting on using his own method of getting there. This was unacceptable, so the eagle was severely disciplined.
>
> And then the fish came home from school and said, "Mom, Dad, I hate school. Swimming is great. Flying is fun if they let me start in the water. But running and climbing? I don't have any legs; and I can't breathe out of the water."
>
> The fish's parents made an appointment for her with the principal who took one look at her progress reports and decreed, "You are so far ahead of the rest of the class in swimming that we're going to let you skip swimming classes and give you private tutoring in running and climbing."
>
> The fish was last seen heading for Canada to request political asylum. The moral of this story is:
>
> Let the fish swim. Let the rabbits run. Let the eagles fly.
>
> We don't want a school of average ducks.
>
> Or, play to people's strengths.

◀ IMPLICATIONS FOR YOU

It's a lesson we learn over and over again. Most of us are unbalanced. We are relatively stronger in one area than another. There is a great temptation to fix others or ourselves by investing time to improve the areas that are relatively less strong. But that's not the way forward.

The better approach is to invest time to improve the areas that are already relatively strong, and find ways to compensate for the gaps. That could be leveraging technology or partnering with someone else. If you are relatively weak at managing operational details, partner with a strong chief operating officer. If you are relatively weak at dealing with people's problems and issues, partner with a strong chief human resources officer. If you are relatively weak at coming up with strategies, partner with a strong chief strategy officer.

There have been some great examples of this through the ages. With Ernest and Julio Gallo, one of them focused on making wine. The other focused on building the business. Wozniak was the technical genius at Apple. Jobs was the one with the consumer vision. At Disney, Frank Wells brought Michael Eisner in to be his boss because he knew he needed a creative genius to complement his business strengths.

This is particularly important with a starter team. Make a conscious effort to bring in people with diverse strengths.

But that's not enough. You also need to bring in people with diverse perspectives.

LOCK IN VALUES

This is the time to lock in your values.

We had a magic moment in the start-up of PrimeGenesis after which we locked in our values. We'd deployed the shield exercise described in Tool 5.3. Each of us had laid out our personal shields with answers to a series of questions. From those we pulled our own individual values and put them on Post-it notes. Then we put the notes on a plate glass window and started grouping them into common themes. It was evening and the fading light from outside was still coming through the window.

Then the light outside faded to the point where it could no longer compete with the light inside the house. The window went black, highlighting the Post-it notes on the window. At that precise moment, each person was looking at the groupings and themes and thinking, "This is exactly the type of organization I'd like to be a part of."

We looked at each other and knew.

From that moment on, we locked our values. From that moment on, everyone who would join our executive onboarding and transition acceleration group PrimeGenesis had to buy into our values—or they could not join.

Our values are

Inspiring
> Committed to excellence and the pursuit of mastery

Results Oriented
> Short terms with urgency; sustainably with long-term view

Integrity beyond Reproach

Lasting Relationships
> Doing what's right for clients over the long run

Team
> Committed to each other, supportive, collaborative

Values are the bedrock of your culture. We're not suggesting you lock in your culture yet. We are suggesting you lock in your values.

Gillian really admired this exercise George did with his team. Often we don't take the time to figure what we stand for, both for our business and for ourselves. By laying out your values at the onset, recruiting, decision making, and planning become much more straightforward. The majority of brands today that have lasted, have done so because they have stayed true to what they stand by.

Innovate by Experimenting

One of the wonderful things about a starter team is that you haven't formed a lot of bad habits yet. Since you're still making things up, experiment. Try things. Make quick, fast, cheap mistakes. Learn from them and move on.

Make Early Sales

Get someone to pay you money for something. When starting PrimeGenesis, George set a series of gates for himself and PrimeGenesis:

- If he couldn't get people to join him as partners in the first six months, he was going to stop.
- If he couldn't get someone to pay for onboarding assistance in the next six months, he was going to stop.
- If he couldn't make a repeat sale in the next six months, he was going to stop.
- If he couldn't see his way to a sustainable revenue stream in the next six months, he was going to stop.

Eleven years later, George still hasn't stopped.

Get Leverage with External Partners

This goes to make, buy, and rent choices. You don't have to do everything your-selves. With a starter team, you don't have the resources to do a lot. You're going to be far better off focusing on the very few things that are absolutely core to solving the problem you've chosen to solve. Outsource the rest.

Make—Do the core yourself. At this point, this is likely the new-to-the-world pieces of solving the problem you're focused on.

Buy—Buy systems and things that are required for you to be successful in the new-to-the-world pieces you're making. You'll want to own them over time because you're likely to adapt them to your needs.

Rent—Beg, borrow, steal, ally, or rent things that support your core activi-ties but are not core. You don't need to be expert at everything. Ally with experts. Let them make money off what they do. Make your money by how you leverage their expertise.

Open Communication

You don't need systems here. You need open, free-flowing communication. Keep the innovation, experimentation gene alive by keeping everyone involved in everything.

No, we're not contradicting our advice to build a team with diverse strengths. We're just saying that everyone can leverage their own strengths to contribute across the enterprise in a starter team.

No walls. No barriers. Open communication.

Know Every Employee

One of our partners is a farmer. He says you should "never name an animal you're going to eat." This applies as you're building your team and are not sure who's really going to contribute. You don't want to get too personal with people you might have to fire.

But the members of your starter team aren't animals. They are your fellow farmers. The risk of having to part ways with one of them is far outweighed by the upside of getting to know them well.

The glue that holds a starter team together is going to be commitment to purpose, values, and relationships. Get to know every single member of the team well.

Draw Some Lines

Since you haven't formed any bad habits yet, this is a good time to start embed-ding some good habits. These will flow from your values. Don't be afraid to start drawing some lines in the sand around the behaviors you value.

Why Overnight Start-up Success is a Myth[4]

It's not quite Brigadoon where each night lasts 100 years, but the overnight start-up success is a myth. Success comes from having a better idea, positioning and resourcing it smarter than your competitors, and working harder than they do over an extended period of time.

Have a Better Idea

Find an unsolved problem. Solve it. Commit to your solution. Commit to continually improving your solution to stay ahead of the inevitable competition. Scott Kurnit, who founded About.com and now heads up New York–based start-up Keep Holdings, put it this way, "In the new world, you're going to have a ton of competitors." You have to be different. If you're copying others, you're "always shooting behind the duck."

Position Better

The pivot point for most start-ups is making sales. Doing that requires a better idea, positioned better. As Triangle Start-Up Factory's Chris Heilvy told George for an earlier article, of course, ideas are important. They are the first step to any great innovation. But they are "not worth (anything) until someone pulls a dollar out of their pockets." Get to real revenue early on.

Kurnit points out that this applies to some, but not all. He says, "You need to generate revenue at the RIGHT time…the biggest don't necessarily turn on revenue early. You have to decide if you're planning to get to first or hit a homerun."

Resource Better

Kurnit reminded George of the funding ladder (Figure 9.1).

The right resources for your start-up depend upon your needs. In today's world there are so many outsourcing opportunities that many companies never need major infrastructure. When Instagram got acquired for $1 billion it had 13 employees. On the other hand Kurnit's Keep Holding raised $43 million before it had any revenue because it needed to scale to a point that would make big company customers comfortable working with them.

Next, get the right resources for your idea, not for some predetermined script.

Work Harder over Time

Overnight successes take six to seven years—if they survive the first three. For example, "overnight success" Twitter struggled for its first two years.

Year 1 is about the dream. It's often a wonderful year as everything is too new to be scary. Expectations are low and mistakes are cheap. As Kurnit put it, at this

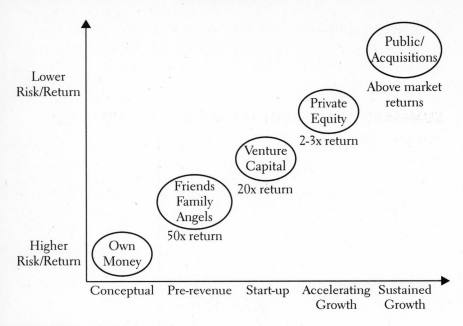

Figure 9.1 The Funding Ladder

point, "People are everything." He is convinced the keys are curiosity and risk taking. Find people who don't want to work in a traditional corporation.

(As an aside, Kurnit laid out the difference between starting a business inside a corporation and outside one. The advantage of starting inside is you don't have to worry about payroll. But, almost by definition, you're going to have people that are less open to risk taking and extra friction with the corporate people around you. If you start inside, isolate yourself as well as possible so you don't get caught up in the corporate culture and endless meetings.)

Year 2 is scary. By then you have "built it." Now you've got to get customers. Often entrepreneurs fall into Paul Grahm's concept of the "trough of despair" at this point. Early failures are good. They cause you to retool, which ends up increasing your chances of success over time. Disaster strikes when you're almost successful. Then you're tempted to keep going instead of either retooling or stopping. This can lead to a death by a thousand cuts—painful.

Year 3 is the breakpoint. Either your business is working or it isn't. If it is, keep going. Keep evolving. Remember, you're still a start-up, still working toward that overnight success several years down the road. If the business isn't working yet, quit. Then start again with an even better idea, positioned and resourced smarter, prepared to work even harder.

We'll give Kurnit the last words of warning:

Start-ups are the innovation point in our economy. The funding structure is set up for the majority of these crazy, audacious ideas to explode . . . in a bad way.

SUMMARY: START WITH ENVIRONMENT AND VALUES

With a "starter" team of less than 10 members (emphasizing environment and values),

- Play where you can solve someone's problem and build the strengths required to solve that problem either in your early team or through external partners.
- Lock in core values.
- Gain early momentum and keep going until it's time to stop.

LEAD TEAMS OF 10 TO 20 LIKE AN EXTENDED FAMILY

Once the team grows beyond the nuclear family of everyone reporting to one leader, the nature of how the team works changes. During this phase, attitude starts to become more important. Get the strategy set, deciding at what you are going to be best in the world, and use that as your guide for how to grow the team and which capabilities to add first. With teams of 10 to 30 people or so, you'll still know everyone and can treat them like extended family. Even so, this is the time to implement rudimentary people-management and operating practices.

All this assumes that the team has already made its where to play choices and has values in place. If so, confirm those choices. If that's not true, start by figuring out whose problem you're going to solve and get the team aligned around where to play.

WHAT MATTERS

The next big question is what matters. Get everyone aligned around the mission and a vision using the tools from Chapter 5.

HOW TO WIN

The critical choice for a team of this size is how to win. Get your strategy and posture set and get your basic culture codified.

MANAGING THE EVOLUTION OF YOUR START-UP'S CORPORATE CULTURE[1]

By the time most organizations start thinking about corporate culture, they already have one. Rick Rudman, cofounder and CEO of cloud marketing software provider Vocus, is unashamedly open that he and his cofounders did not plan their culture. It emerged. But, as it emerged, they made conscious choices about what to keep and what to evolve.

Over the past six years, Vocus has acquired seven companies, and the cultures of those companies it acquired have not combined to form an entirely new culture. Rather, Vocus carefully selected organizations that fit into its already established culture. I recently spoke with Rudman and here's what he had to say about the processes behind building the Vocus corporate culture.

WHY CULTURE MATTERS TODAY

Rudman is convinced that corporate culture is the only truly sustainable competitive advantage. But it's rarely the first advantage of a startup. Vocus' founders set out to "write incredible software." They chose to "take the business seriously, but not ourselves seriously." From the start, they worked hard and took time during the day to have some fun, like stopping by Toys "R" Us to bring some toys back to the office. Even their first official planning session consisted of the company's eight employees working on the train on the way to an evening in Atlantic City. (Think Las Vegas meets the Jersey Shore.)

That "became a culture that worked," said Rudman. People were attracted by that culture and "became a part of us." Many successful start-ups will market their internal culture through social media and their websites. Why does everyone seem to want to work for Google? Because they have done an amazing job at marketing their culture outward.

THE BUILDING BLOCKS OF THE VOCUS CULTURE

Now, Vocus' culture is one of their sources of pride. In terms of the components that make up the Vocus culture, let's break it down in terms of BRAVE:

Vocus' *environment* speaks volumes. They have laid out their 93,000 square foot corporate office to have the look and feel of a town (Seaside, Florida, to be specific). As Rudman explains, it has a main street for people to stroll on, a coffee shop for people to escape to, an oasis for food, a fitness center, and a "bored" room for formal meetings. (Yes. *Bored* is spelled right.)

Their *values* haven't changed much. They still drive "open communication and teamwork while allowing opportunity for individual achievements," "integrity," "customer-focus," and working and playing hard.

Vocus' employees share the same *attitude* of taking work seriously without taking themselves too seriously.

The environment, values, and attitude inform their *relationships*, guiding, if not defining, the way they work together.

All of this leads to a set of *behaviors* that make it a fun place to work, but where employees are able to make a large impact on their customers. To support the

Vocus way of life, the company has several internal committees dedicated to cultivating its culture. The It's All about You Committee enhances employee work lives by introducing programs like on-site basketball tournaments and group yoga classes, and the It's Not All about You Committee pushes employees out into the community to volunteer.

SUSTAINING AND BUILDING CULTURE

Rudman works very hard to sustain and improve the Vocus culture. He has chosen to acquire smaller companies and fold them into the Vocus culture. One example is iContact, which was a larger acquisition than normal. Rudman shared that folding iContact in took "a lot of proactive work," which included building a new environment for them similar to Vocus' headquarters, changing their language and acronyms, and helping them become part of the Vocus family.

> Implications for you: In many ways, culture is a shared set of BRAVE preferences. People joining a start-up need to buy into the founders' preferences. Of course, culture evolves—but it rarely shifts quickly. And above all else, the right fit is what matters most.

TEAM EXPANSION

The strategy choices are particularly important in guiding the team expansion. Up until this point, the team has probably been acquiring the best athletes it could—hopefully with complementary strengths. Now, armed with choices around at what you are going to be best in the world, you can focus on building those strengths.

PEOPLE MANAGEMENT AND OPERATING PRACTICES

In some ways, fun time is over. A team of 20 people cannot operate the way a team of 5 people can. You'll need to start implementing some of the operating practices described in Chapters 7 and 8 on relationships and behaviors. No need to go full bore and implement them all. Just the ones that make it easier for you all to be productive together.

In particular, it may be time to start implementing performance reviews.

Now is the time to start teaching your new team members how to think like entrepreneurs. People in teams of less than 10 people have to think like entrepreneurs to survive. As teams get larger, some of that gets lost. Don't let it.

FEEDBACK

As part of those practices, be more and more conscious about providing on-the-spot feedback to keep all moving in the same direction. People who are close enough to you to know what you're thinking in a team of less than 10 people may need you to be a little more explicit as the team grows in size.

One idea is to start looking at different interpretations as one approach to conflict resolution: "Can you see how when you say x it can be interpreted as y?"

SUMMARY: EVOLVE ATTITUDE

With a team operating like an extended family of 10 to 30 members (emphasizing attitude),

- Choose what you are going to be best in the world at.
- Let that choice guide team expansion priorities.
- Agree on the main tenets of your culture and start implementing operational practices to embed those tenets.

IF YOU'RE LEADING MORE THAN 30 PEOPLE, HIERARCHY IS YOUR FRIEND

Once teams grow beyond 30 people or so, you need to get over your natural abhorrence of hierarchy and start substituting some organizational and operating processes for your ability to know everyone on the team. At this stage, lead with relating and behaviors (how to connect, what impact). Work on the organization. Put in place enabling practices to scale. And remember the number one job of the leader is to own and reinforce vision and values. This gets ever more important (and complicated) as the organization grows.

WORK ON THE ORGANIZATION

With a small team, everyone is in sales. Everyone is in marketing. Everyone is in customer service. Actually, everyone does everything part of the time. They back each other up, hopefully driven by the same mission. As teams grow beyond 30 people, specialization is both tolerated and required on the way to building differentiated expertise.

As the leader, your job is to inspire and enable. What happens with teams of over 30 is that enabling requires more sophisticated, more complex work. It's no longer sufficient for you to be part of the organization, doing your job and helping others as needed. Now you need to spend time working on the organization, doing less and less yourself, creating a hierarchy in a way that enables open communication and free-flowing ideas.

ENABLING PRACTICES

It gets worse. As the organization grows, you can't be there or be close by guiding everything along the way. You need to put in place enabling practices to

205

take your place. These practices initially steer people in the right direction. Over time, they embed habits of excellence and become part of the culture.

EMBEDDING OPERATIONAL PRACTICES[1]

You can start a cultural change with organizational changes or strategic changes. But until the operations change, nothing will stick. This is often the most difficult part of the change process because operations involve ingrained habits, practices, and systems. This is where the sacred cows hang out. This is the domain of long-tenured employees—who have seen change agents come and go.

But fear not; it can be done. Don't give up. Find the chinks in the armor. Find the ambiguities and drive your cultural change right through them. It's worth the effort because corporate culture is the only truly sustainable competitive advantage.

Equifax's Andy Bodea provides a great example of how to do this. He leveraged the revolution in the technological environment as his platform for change, worked with his team to envision a more effective and efficient reality, and drove the steps in his call to action relentlessly over time.

Platform for Change

Global operations had been viewed as more of a support function within Equifax. But the information technology revolution meant that Equifax had to find ways to manage data more efficiently and effectively if it was to keep up with its competition. This gave Bodea an important external platform for change.

> To strengthen the customer relationship and drive more revenue growth we needed to create greater scale.

Envisioned Future State

What Bodea envisioned was a highly customer-centric and more robust Equifax experience, driving growth through operations. He saw opportunities to create and leverage direct links between operations and the customers—links that would generate efficiencies and insight to fuel new sales, growth initiatives, and industry solutions. Essentially he wanted to turn operations into a competitive advantage.

Call to Action

To achieve this vision, Bodea knew he had to

1. Get buy-in from leadership. (As part of this, Bodea's leadership needed to know and understand his commitment to lead this—from the front, by example.)

2. Assemble/rejuvenate the team. "Building a team that combined the old and the new was critical to our success. It was critical for me as a leader to not underestimate the people part, getting people to engage, be willing to support and sustain the change. Strategy and execution has to be joined by a very strong psychological conversion of beliefs, from the old patterns to the new."

3. Develop and communicate a strategic plan "grounded in reality"—explainable on one page.

4. Identify a set of initiatives and refresh the list annually and quarterly as needed to meet the targets.

5. Put specific goals in place (revenues and margins)—built into the budgets of business units and functions so there was a shared commitment to making things happen. "This is a critical element."

6. Prioritize the needs, the requirements, and the opportunities.

7. Ensure organizational clarity and alignment through nested operating rhythms:
   • One-on-one with direct reports once per quarter to look at prior quarter accomplishments and next quarter's priorities.
   • The same thing on a monthly basis plus business metrics.
   • Look at initiatives' progress every other week.

These steps create an opportunity to see what's going on and influence it along the way instead of waiting too long.

> Critical to our journey was a relentless focus on Equifax's overarching strategy, grounded in a clear and real vision that was supported by an operating model sensitive to the Business Unit nuances but had been stressed tested and forged into razor sharp rigor and a bias for speed and execution.

The results have been terrific: a world-class integrated data platform; expanded consumer and customer databases; online, self-service systems; strengthened product fulfillment; new ways of onboarding customers more quickly; and cultural acceptance of a shared services model leading to 13 consecutive quarters of double-digit million dollar annual operating margins. Equifax's credit score is strong!

VISION AND VALUES

The number one job of leader is to reinforce vision and values. This gets more important as an organization grows. You need to become more and more of a champion and spokesperson and less and less of a doer. You need to drive the vision and values over and over and over again. You'll get bored and tired of it way before it begins to get any traction with the newer members of your team. When that happens, take a break and start all over again.

SUMMARY: TEAM EVOLUTION

With a "starter" team of less than 10 members (emphasizing environment and values):

- Play where you can solve someone's problem and build the strengths required to solve that problem either in your early team or through external partners.
- Lock in core values.
- Gain early momentum and keep going until it's time to stop.

With a team operating like an extended family of 10 to 30 members (emphasizing attitude):

- Choose what you are going to be best in the world at.
- Let that choice guide team expansion priorities.
- Agree about the main tenets of your culture and start implementing operational practices to embed those tenets.

With a team of over 30 members starting to embrace hierarchy (emphasizing relationships and behaviors):

- Work on the organization.
- Put in place enabling practices to scale.
- Reinforce vision and values—the number one job of a leader.

NOTE

The 48 tools printed in this book are also available in a customizable format at www.onboardingtools.com. (See the First-Time Leader page.) We will be regularly updating these tools and adding videos and additional material on that page to give you the benefit of our latest thinking.

NOTES

CHAPTER 1 OVERVIEW: CONGRATULATIONS! IT'S GREAT TO BE A LEADER. YOU'VE EARNED IT. AND YOUR NEW JOB IS GOING TO BE A WILD RIDE

1. Anne Fisher, "New Job? Get a Head Start Now," *Fortune*, February 17, 2012.

2. Per Michael Porter in *Competitive Analysis* (New York: Free Press, 1985).

CHAPTER 2 TAKE CHARGE OF YOUR NEW TEAM

1. Adapted from George Bradt's Forbes.com article on the subject—February 25, 2011.

2. See Brene Brown's TED Talk, "The Power of Vulnerability," Houston, June 2010.

3. From George Bradt's Forbes.com article on the subject—March 2, 2011.

4. From George Bradt's Forbes.com article on the subject—May 15, 2012.

5. Fisher, "New Job? Get a Head Start Now."

6. From George Bradt's Forbes.com article on the subject—December 12, 2012.

7. Shakespeare's newly crowned Henry V in *Henry IV*, Act V, Scene v: "Presume not that I am the thing I was; For God doth know, so shall the world perceive, That I have turn'd away my former self . . ."

8. This was originally said by Sun-Tzu, 400 BC, despite most of us remembering it as one of the things Michael Corleone's father taught him "here in this room" in *The Godfather II*.

9. This was adapted from Kevin P. Coyne and Edward J. Coyne's article "Surviving Your New CEO," *Harvard Business Review*, May 2007, and then expanded.

CHAPTER 4   ENVIRONMENT

1. Steven Covey, *The 7 Habits of Highly Effective People* (New York: Simon & Schuster, 1989).

2. From Tony Hsieh, *Delivering Happiness: A Path to Profits, Passion, and Purpose* (Mundelein, IL: Round Table Comics, 2012). Pages 67–68.

3. Ibid.

4. From George Bradt's Forbes.com article on the subject—November 21, 2012.

5. From George Bradt's Forbes.com article on the subject—November 7, 2012.

6. From George Bradt's Forbes.com article on the subject—May 8, 2013.

CHAPTER 5   VALUES

1. From George Bradt's Forbes.com article on the subject—April 10, 2013.

CHAPTER 6   ATTITUDE

1. From George Bradt's Forbes.com article on the subject—May 29, 2013.

2. Posted on LinkedIn, May 21, 2013.

3. George Bradt on Forbes.com, February 13, 2013.

4. See Edgar Schein, *Organizational Culture and Leadership* (San Francisco: Jossey-Bass, 1985).

5. From George Bradt's Forbes.com article on the subject—September 28, 2011.

CHAPTER 7   RELATIONSHIPS

1. From Peter Senge, Art Kleiner, Charlotte Roberts, Richard Ross, and Bryan Smith, *The Fifth Discipline Fieldbook* (London: Nicholas Brealey Publishing, 1994).

2. Meaghan M. McDermott, "Brizard Takes City School District's Reins Today," *Rochester Democrat and Chronicle*, January 2, 2008. (Brizard later moved on to head up Chicago's schools.)

3. From George Bradt's Forbes.com article on the subject—March 9, 2011.

4. Much of this section is based on work by Sandy Linver and her company Speakeasy, also laid out in her book *Speak and Get Results* (New York: Simon & Schuster, 1994).

5. Ibid.

6. From George Bradt's Forbes.com article on the subject—January 11, 2012.

7. Joseph Campbell, *The Hero with a Thousand Faces* (New York: Pantheon, 1949).

8. From George Bradt's Forbes.com article on the subject—February 22, 2012.

9. www.greatplacetowork.com/best-companies/100-best-companies-to-work-for.

10. From George Bradt and Mary Vonnegut, *Onboarding: How to Get Your New Employees Up to Speed in Half the Time* (New York: John Wiley & Sons, 2009). Pages 55–56.

11. Ibid., page 56.

12. From George Bradt's Forbes.com article on the subject—December 19, 2012.

13. Marcus Buckingham and Donald Clifton, *Now Discover Your Strengths* (New York: Free Press, 2001).

14. Covey, *The 7 Habits of Highly Effective People*.

15. G. T. Doran, "There's a S.M.A.R.T. Way to Write Management's Goals and Objectives," *Management Review* 70, no. 11 (1981, AMA Forum): 35–36.

16. From George Bradt's Forbes.com article on the subject—June 20, 2012.

17. From George Bradt's Forbes.com article on the subject—September 18, 2012.

CHAPTER 8   BEHAVIORS

1. From George Bradt's Forbes.com article on the subject—November 29, 2012.

2. From George Bradt's Forbes.com article on the subject—March 23, 2011.

3. Methodology was developed in conjunction with a number of people at the American Red Cross and especially Becky McCorry, disaster operations center director; Chris Saeger, director of performance improvement; and Armond Mascelli, VP of disaster operations. It would be hard to find

a group of people more closely aligned around a more meaningful shared purpose. It has been one of my life's great privileges to be able to work with them — George.

4. Professor Leonard Lodish, lecture at the University of Pennsylvania, Wharton School, 1984.

5. Attributed to Charles Darwin.

6. John Harrald argues the need for both discipline (structure, doctrine, process) and agility (creativity, improvisation, adaptability) in "Agility and Discipline: Critical Success Factors for Disaster Response," *ANNALS of the American Academy of Political and Social Science* 604 (2006): 256.

7. Ibid.

8. Chris Saeger, discussion at American Red Cross, May 2010.

9. From George Bradt's Forbes.com article on the subject — January 30, 2013.

CHAPTER 9   WITH TEAMS OF LESS THAN 10 PEOPLE, ADOPT A START-UP MIND-SET

1. From George Bradt's Forbes.com article on the subject — October 16, 2013.

2. From George Bradt's Forbes.com article on the subject — June 12, 2013.

3. From George Bradt's Forbes.com article on the subject — December 7, 2011.

4. From George Bradt's Forbes.com article on the subject — October 9, 2013.

CHAPTER 10   LEAD TEAMS OF 10 TO 20 LIKE AN EXTENDED FAMILY

1. From George Bradt's Forbes.com article on the subject — March 20, 2013.

CHAPTER 11   IF YOU'RE LEADING MORE THAN 30 PEOPLE, HIERARCHY IS YOUR FRIEND

1. From George Bradt's Forbes.com article on the subject — March 21, 2012.

REFERENCES

Bradt, George. 2011–2013. *The New Leader's Playbook*. Articles on Forbes.com.

Bradt, George, and Ed Bancroft. 2010. *The Total Onboarding Program*. San Francisco: Wiley/Pfeifer.

Bradt, George, Jayme Check, and Jorge Pedraza. 2011. *The New Leader's 100-Day Action Plan*. 3rd ed. Hoboken, NJ: John Wiley & Sons.

Bradt, George, and Mary Vonnegut. 2009. *Onboarding: How to Get Your New Employees Up to Speed in Half the Time*. Hoboken, NJ: John Wiley & Sons.

Bradt, George, and Mary Vonnegut. 2012. *The New Job 100-Day Plan*. New York: PrimeGenesis.

Buckingham, Marcus, and Donald Clifton. 2001. *Now Discover Your Strengths*. New York: Free Press.

Campbell, Joseph. 1949. *The Hero with a Thousand Faces*. New York: Pantheon.

Covey, Steven. 1989. *The 7 Habits of Highly Effective People*. New York: Simon & Schuster.

Coyne, Kevin P., and Edward J. Coyne. 2007. "Surviving Your New CEO." *Harvard Business Review*, May.

Doran, G. T. 1981. "There's a S.M.A.R.T. Way to Write Management's Goals and Objectives." *Management Review* 70, no. 11 (AMA Forum): 35–36.

Fisher, Anne. 2012. "New Job? Get a Head Start Now." *Fortune*, February 17.

Groysberg, Boris, Andrew Hill, and Toby Johnson. 2010. "Which of These People Is Your Future CEO?" *Harvard Business Review*, November.

Harrald, John. 2006. "Agility and Discipline: Critical Success Factors for Disaster Response." *The ANNALS of the American Academy of Political and Social Science* 604: 256.

Heiman, Stephen, and Diane Sanchez. 1998. *The New Strategic Selling*. New York: Warner Books.

Hsieh, Tony. 2012. *Delivering Happiness: A Path to Profits, Passion, and Purpose*. Mundelein, IL: Round Table Comics.

Linver, Sandy. 1994. *Speak and Get Results*. New York: Simon & Schuster.

Lodish, Leonard. 1984. Class discussion, University of Pennsylvania, Wharton School.

McDermott, Meaghan M. 2008. "Brizard Takes City School District's Reins Today." *Rochester Democrat and Chronicle*, January 2.

Schein, Edgar. 1985. *Organizational Culture and Leadership*. San Francisco: Jossey-Bass.

Senge, Peter, Art Kleiner, Charlotte Roberts, Richard Ross, and Bryan Smith. 1994. *The Fifth Discipline Fieldbook*. London: Nicholas Brealey Publishing.

Smith, Bruay. 1994. *The Fifth Discipline Field Book*. Boston: Nicholas Brealey.

NOTE

The 48 tools printed in this book are also available in a customizable format at www.onboardingtools.com. (See the First-Time Leader page.) We will be regularly updating these tools and adding videos and additional material on that page to give you the benefit of our latest thinking.

ABOUT THE AUTHORS

George Bradt has a unique perspective on transformational leadership based on his experience as an executive, consultant, and writer. He progressed through sales, marketing, and general management roles in North America, Europe, and Asia at companies including Unilever, Procter & Gamble, Coca-Cola, and J.D. Power's Power Information Network spin-off, as chief executive.

Now he is a principal of CEO Connection and managing director of PrimeGenesis, the executive onboarding and transition acceleration group he founded in 2003. Since then, George and PrimeGenesis have reduced new leader failure rates from 40 percent to 10 percent, by helping them and their teams deliver *better results faster*.

George is a graduate of Harvard and Wharton (MBA) and the author of five books on onboarding, including the best-selling *New Leader's 100-Day Action Plan*; a weekly column on Forbes.com, "The New Leader's Playbook"; two *Back-to-School Chats* books on parenting; and four musical plays (book, lyrics, and music).

Onboarding books authored or co-authored by George Bradt:

First-Time Leader (John Wiley & Sons, 2014)
The New Job 100-Day Plan (PrimeGenesis, 2012)
The Total Onboarding Program: An Integrated Approach (Wiley/Pfeiffer, 2010)
Onboarding: How to Get Your New Employees Up to Speed in Half the Time (John Wiley & Sons, 2009)
The New Leader's 100-Day Action Plan (John Wiley & Sons, 2006, 2009, 2011)

George can be reached at gbradt@primegenesis.com.

Gillian Davis brings a new generation's view to leadership based on her involvement with recruiting, coaching, online marketing, and start-ups, while growing up in Montreal.

Gillian is now based in London, working with first time leaders to inspire and enable their new teams. Using her unique approach, Gillian drives businesses forward by helping them attract, recruit, and retain talent.

Gillian can be reached at Gillian@firsttimeleader.tv or @gilliandavis07.

INDEX

217